TO BOLDLY GO
RARE PHOTOS FROM THE TOS SOUNDSTAGE

SEASON ONE

Gerald Gurian

Minkatek Press
Las Vegas, Nevada

LIBRARY OF CONGRESS CATALOGUING-IN-PUBLICATION DATA
Gurian, Gerald
To Boldly Go - Rare Photos from the TOS Soundstage: Season One /
Gerald Gurian; with a foreword by Marc Cushman;
Edited by Marc Cushman, Sondra Johnson and Andrew Johnson

ISBN 978-0-6926438-5-3

First Edition ... March 10, 2016

Library of Congress Control Number: 2016902670

This book is a work of journalism, protected under the First Amendment, and is not endorsed, sponsored, or affiliated with CBS Studios Inc. or the "Star Trek®" franchise. The *Star Trek®* trademarks, logos, and related names are owned by CBS Studios Inc. and are used under "fair use" guidelines.

*No part of this book may be reproduced or transmitted in any form
or by any means, electronic or mechanical, including photocopying
or recording, or by any information storage and retrieval system,
without permission in writing from the author.*

Cover design: Gerald Gurian and Susan Osborn
Interior design: Gerald Gurian and Marc Cushman

Manufactured in the United States of America

Minkatek Press
Las Vegas, Nevada

Front cover: Barry Mason slates the starship U.S.S. Enterprise filming miniature alongside the SS Botany Bay spacecraft model on the soundstage of Film Effects of Hollywood, 1966.

To my brother Bernard, for a lifetime of love, support and encouragement,

and in memory of our beloved parents Anne and Joseph,

and in memory of our dear brother Steven.

To Gene Roddenberry and the entire production cast and crew of The Original Series,

for their tireless efforts in creating an exceptional work which has inspired millions.

To Marc Cushman, for his friendship, encouragement and invaluable assistance

in making the creation of this edition a reality.

To all of my fellow fans of Star Trek, who keep the worldwide phenomenon alive and

strong, may you all Live Long and Prosper.

Acknowledgments

In assembling any list of the noteworthy individuals who have positively influenced a work that is primarily concerned with the *Star Trek* television series, I think it is imperative to acknowledge the exceptional team of cast and production crew that boldly brought forth that magnificent creation onto our television screens and into our hearts in September of 1966. So I would feel great remiss if I did not begin this page by saluting the dedicated efforts of the following group for so positively influencing and inspiring the lives of myself and millions of fans. I apologize in advance for not including everyone behind the cameras or indeed the hundreds of guest actors that all played a role in making the series so remarkable:

Majel Barrett, John D. F. Black, Mary Black, Wah Ming Chang, Gene L. Coon, Alexander Courage, Douglas S. Cramer, Joseph D'Agosta, Marc Daniels, Kellam De Forest, John M. Dwyer, Irving A. Feinberg, Jerry Fielding, Jerry Finnerman, Dorothy "D.C." Fontana, Al Francis, Fred Freiberger, Gerald Fried, Doug Grindstaff, Walter "Matt" Jefferies, Robert H. Justman, DeForest Kelley, Walter Koenig, John Meredyth Lucas, Margaret Makau, Eddie Milkis, Michael Minor, Nichelle Nichols, Leonard Nimoy, Gregg Peters, Joseph Pevney, Fred B. Phillips, Gene Roddenberry, Jim Rugg, Ralph Senensky, William Shatner, Bruce Shoengarth, Arthur H. Singer, Herbert F. Solow, George Takei, William Ware Theiss, Fabien D. Tordjmann, Charles Washburn, Albert Whitlock, Grace Lee Whitney

For their years of friendship, kindness, inspiration and encouragement, and enjoyable interaction on all things Star Trek that has served to continuously reinvigorate my passion and enthusiasm for the franchise, I must thank a list of wonderful folks from many venues. This would include my friends at Jacobs Brown Press and CBS Consumer Products as well as those who are cherished associates within Star Trek fandom and in the field of Star Trek prop and costume collecting, and especially those friends that share my passion for Desilu film clip collecting and restoration - to all of you who have so generously shared your passion, knowledge and companionship, or have given support and encouragement in other meaningful ways, I owe you all special thanks:

Mark Alfred, Mark Altman, Paula M. Block, Christopher P. Beamish, John D. F. Black, Scott R. Brooks, James A. Brown, George A. Brozak, Jeff Castillo, John A. Castillo, James Cawley, Brian Chanes, Bobby Clark, Randy Combs, Marian Cordry, Duane L. Crandall, Marc Cushman, Desi DosSantos, Doug Drexler, Harlan Ellison, Terry J. Erdmann, Bernard Gurian, Alan R. Holland, Huston Huddleston, Jarrod Hunt, Darrell Hyde, Robert "Jake" Jacobs, Greg Jein, Andrew Johnson, Sondra Johnson, Penny Juday, Steven Jay Kates, Sean Kenney, Kevin A. Kohls, William Krewson, Jon Laxton, Mallory Levitt, BarBara Luna, Michael Makkreel, Bonnie Heim Malmat, Scott Mantz, Don Marshall, Barry Mason, Rachel Mason, Robert J. Miller, Minka, Martin Netter, Nichelle Nichols, Adam Nimoy, Robert O'Connell, Michael Okuda, Bob Olsen, Susan Osborn, Eddie Paskey, Elaine Peschke, Alec Peters, Carolan Prisco, David B. Rodier, Joe Sacco, Nadine Sacco, Donna Sakaida, Adam L. Schneider, Leslie Schneider, Nick Shone, William Smith, Nikki Stafford, Rick Sternbach, Mark Stevens, Kipp Teague, Thomas C. Tucker, John Van Citters, Deepa Vedapudi, Sairam Vedapudi, Fred Walder, Gene Winfield, Anthony Zabiegalski, Paolo Zanghellini

Table of Contents

Foreword

Sometimes we get lucky.

In early 2013, as I was putting the finishing touches on the first of a three-book set documenting the making of the original *Star Trek* series, my publisher began searching for images to help illustrate the story. Of course, the first call was to CBS, the current owners of that first *Star Trek* series. CBS didn't respond as quickly as my publisher in a hurry needed, so we looked for other photo options – pictures that would be considered in the public domain. That's when we came across Gerald Gurian by way of his website, *startrekpropauthority.com*. There we saw fantastic pictures from the original series – things I'd never seen before … and I'm a fan! There were outtakes, behind-the-scenes shots, NBC and Desilu publicity photos from the 1960s, and Lincoln Enterprises film trims.

If you don't know what Lincoln Enterprises is, shame on you. Any *Star Trek* fan worth his weight in tribbles knows about Lincoln Enterprises. It was Gene Roddenberry's mail-order company, started in 1968 with the help of John and Bjo Trimble, and set up to sell *Star Trek* scripts, photos, and film trims, among other collectibles, with the proceeds intended to finance "Save *Star Trek*" campaigns. And make Gene some money. Back then, if you wrote a fan letter to *Star Trek*, or to NBC about *Star Trek* (which were often forwarded to the *Star Trek* offices), you soon received a Lincoln Enterprises catalogue in the mail. I was fourteen when I received mine, and was happily surprised to learn that I could purchase *Star Trek* scripts, pictures and film trims. The trims were the actual pieces of color film snipped from longer strips of film while the episodes were being cut together. Many of these trims showed the scenes being slated – the clapboard shots – in which a crew member (usually Bill McGovern) would stand before the camera with a slate on which was written the episode title, filming date, scene number, and which camera "take" they were about to shoot. Behind this person you saw the cast members, and guest stars, and various sets, all waiting to become part of a classic *Star Trek* episode.

Jump forward a few decades or more: As the color was fading on those pieces of film, some of those who bought and saved them began to sell their trims on eBay or at conventions, or through other means. That is how collectors like Gerald Gurian ended up owning thousands of film trims. In Gerald's case, it may even be tens of thousands! … as well as NBC, Desilu and Paramount promotional pictures, and other collectibles.

Long story short, Jacobs/Brown Press contacted Gerald on my behalf and asked if he'd be willing to provide images for our book series. That's why I say that sometimes we get lucky. Gerald said "yes."

I couldn't have asked for better pictures for my books – and Gerald provided us with about 1,000, spread over the three-book series. If you've seen *These Are the Voyages*, you understand why I feel these are absolutely the perfect images. These books don't just tell the story of the making of *Star Trek*, they serve as a sort of time machine, whisking the reader back to the production offices and the writers room and the soundstages of *Star Trek* during the years 1964 (for the making of "The Cage") through 1969, when "Turnabout Intruder," the last episode of *TOS* ("The Original Series"), was filmed. To accomplish this, I used the memos from Gene Roddenberry, Gene Coon, Bob Justman, Dorothy

Fontana, and Stan Robinson at NBC, among others, as well as production schedules, budgets, and interviews taken on the set from that time, augmented by newer interviews I conducted, and anything else I could find to help switch the time machine on.

Now that you know, I ask you – what pictures could possibly serve a book series such as this better than film trims showing Bill McGovern slating a shot? Reading about what was happening as the scenes were being filmed, and then looking at those pictures of Bill about to clap his slate, one cannot help but feel that they were there, standing on the sidelines. It worked beautifully. And all because CBS didn't call back right away and Gerald Gurian said "yes."

As I said, sometimes we get lucky.

I should tell you that some of the pictures we used came from other collectors (all acknowledged in the book series) – maybe 10% of them – but even in those instances, it was Gerald who did the restoration and enhancement so that the images would translate well to print.

The story might have ended there except for one thing – some of you who bought those books then wrote to us. You wanted more pictures, and bigger pictures, and, God forbid, color pictures. Well, that couldn't happen. These books are true tomes – over 600 pages each! That's a lot of paper, and ink. If the pictures were bigger or in color and on glossy paper, we'd have to charge more than you would probably want to spend. But, as the theme of this foreword keeps telling us, sometimes we get lucky.

In late 2015, Gerald Gurian sent me a manuscript of a picture book he was preparing and felt that my feedback on it would be of benefit. The manuscript included many of those pictures he had provided for my books – but bigger and, in many cases, in vivid color. It also contained pictures that I had never seen before, so perhaps you haven't seen them before either. You see, Gerald has continued to collect. And, bless him, he continues to want to share his collection with us fans.

I am a very fortunate person for having met Gerald Gurian. I like him. And I've been given a guided tour through the rooms that store his various *Star Trek* collections. And now you get to have a guided tour by Gerald through some of those rooms too.

Now you can say it too. Sometimes we get lucky.

Marc Cushman
February, 2016.

Preface

Some of my earliest childhood memories hearken back to my deep love of *Star Trek*. I can distinctly recall, as a child of only 5 or 6 years old, delving into a kitchen cabinet drawer to extract a package of shiny, silver colored aluminum foil, that was of course intended to safeguard foods, and instead using almost the entire roll to build up the superstructure of my handmade U.S.S. Enterprise starship model - the skeleton for which I had carefully constructed by bending and reshaping a number of handy metal coat hangers. To my parents credit, for which I was quite thankful, they tolerated the non-standard requisition of the foil and the hangers in the name of the United Federation of Planets and allowed me to enjoy my shiny new creation without any reprimands for possibly allowing a sandwich or other perishable food item to go without a proper wrapping. I wasn't particularly concerned that my ship's hull color would differ somewhat from the real thing that was shown on television each week -- to me, my version was a perfect vehicle to further fuel my imagination for all things *Star Trek*. As I dashed through the hallways and rooms of my family's one and a half story red brick house in Toronto, Canada, with my Enterprise model held up high, I was no longer confined to the trappings of everyday life in the suburbs of a mid-20th century city but was exploring the furthest boundaries of the Federation with Captain Kirk and crew.

Of course, at such a young age, I imagine that it was the action and adventure inherent in *Star Trek*, combined with the futuristic technology and the stunning alien creatures - like the hideous M-113 Salt Vampire or the menacing Gorn Captain - which captured my interest and caused a fascination with the series, along with some exciting special effects which were certainly leading edge at the time for '60s television.

Yet as I grew older, I discovered that my enjoyment and passion for the series only deepened. Which speaks to, I believe, one of the significant reasons for the phenomenal success of *Star Trek* -- that it truly appealed to all age groups and across all demographics of fandom. It delivered not only the high paced action and special effects necessary to captivate the youngest of audiences but also provided highly intelligent and thought provoking science fiction - a dramatic departure from virtually all other televised entertainment programs of its day - to thoroughly excite an adult audience as well.

As a teenager, I remember racing home from school in anticipation of watching the 5:00 pm broadcast of *Star Trek* on channel 9, CFTO-TV, where it played in syndication during the early '70s in Toronto. I looked forward to watching all of those broadcasts with utmost pleasure; even though - as time went by - I realized that I had seen those same episodes perhaps 7 or 8 or 10 or more times in previous airings. And as if the Monday through Friday showings were not enough; I recall recording the soundtracks of the episodes, carefully pausing my tape recorder during the commercials, so that I could play back the audio of those cherished missions whenever I desired without regard to the fixed television broadcast schedule. At that time, I took a great deal of pride in my ability to instantly recall the specific stardates and planet names that were associated with particular events in the 79 original series episodes; and I was able to describe all of the intricacies of starship operations and technology at a minute level of detail, as well as quote many significant passages of dialogue from the broadcasts without error. Needless to say, with the passage of several decades, although my passion for the Original Series remains strong - my capacity to keep all of those facts at the tip of my tongue has greatly diminished.

One aspect of *Star Trek* that my adolescent self certainly appreciated to a vastly greater degree than my 5 year old self - who was likely oblivious to this facet of the show - would have to be the endless array of tremendously beautiful and frequently scantily clad guest actresses that Gene Roddenberry and company saw fit to incorporate into the weekly telecasts. Who can forget the mesmerizing dances of Susan Oliver and Yvonne Craig as green Orion slave girls (also known as Orion animal women) or the compelling performances of the beautiful Angelique Pettyjohn as Shahna, France Nuyen as Elaan, Louise Sorel as Rayna, Jill Ireland as Leila, BarBara Luna as Marlena, or Sherry Jackson as Andrea - just to name a few! And we must not leave out the lovely Nichelle Nichols and Grace Lee Whitney from the recurring cast - who I must confess were both the subject of boyhood crushes all those years ago. Certainly the multitude of beautiful women with exotic costumes featured in the episodes was another contributing factor to the immense popularity of the series. And even now, I can report that some of the most frequently visited posts on my extensive *Star Trek* art and production history website, called *startrekpropauthority.com*, are a pair of photo studies that were created as a tribute to the beautiful women of *Star Trek*.

In April of 2002, I was honored to see an article that I wrote discussing some of my memorable personal encounters with several Original Series cast members published in the ECW Press paperback "Trekkers: True Stories By Fans For Fans", edited by Nikki Stafford. In an attempt to explain the amazing worldwide popularity of the franchise and the most significant aspects of the show that appealed to me, I wrote: "Aside from providing superb and exciting action entertainment ... *Star Trek* provided a bona fide cast of larger-than-life heroes espousing core values such as honesty, integrity, loyalty, bravery, compassion, self-sacrifice, and perseverance despite seemingly insurmountable obstacles. While other television series of the times were caught up in ethnic stereotypes, *Star Trek* presented a bold vision of a multi-national, multiracial crew operating in harmony and bound by their common thread of humanity. By the 24th century, we were assured that Earth would have solved the devastating problems of mass poverty, hunger, and disease, and mankind would no longer be divided by petty politics or racial prejudice." Indeed, I still feel that this overwhelmingly positive portrait of humanity, with its optimistic portrayal of mankind's future, is perhaps the single most important factor in the global appeal of the franchise. One particular interview that I saw with William Shatner comes to mind, in which he remarked that whenever he was acting in the role of Captain Kirk, he attempted to infuse the character with what he termed was "a nobility of spirit". I think that phrase perfectly captures the nature of not only his performance but those of his primary co-stars - Leonard Nimoy and DeForest Kelley - and that their combined on-screen performances and exceptional chemistry together certainly resonated very powerfully with worldwide audiences.

Today, I would add that, any discussion of the factors which contributed to the great success of *Star Trek* would be incomplete if there was no mention of how the show truly witnessed a unique collaboration of exceptionally talented individuals from all the major disciplines involved in television production - and thus was able to benefit from not only the superlative work of the actors in front of the cameras, but also the brilliance of folks such as Gene Roddenberry, Gene L. Coon, Dorothy Fontana, John D. F. Black and Bob Justman in scriptwriting and script review; the genius of Matt Jefferies in Production Design who created much of the look and feel of the starship sets as well as the many alien worlds that the Enterprise crew encountered; the magnificent work of William Ware Theiss in Costume Design who developed all of the starfleet uniforms and all of the alien attire seen in the 79 classic episodes; the groundbreaking and truly inspired work of Jerry Finnerman in cinematography, especially for his signature efforts in set lighting; and the immense talent of Wah Chang that was reflected in his many prop and alien contributions to the series, including the communicator, the tricorder, the Gorn, the Balok puppet, the M-113 Salt Vampire and numerous other creations. And let us not forget the extraordinary work of those such as Alexander Courage, Gerald Fried, Jerry Fielding, Sol Kaplan and others for their unforgettable musical compositions that perfectly accentuated the activity unfolding before our eyes. All of the members of that one-of-a-kind production team certainly cared deeply about the show and committed themselves to producing a program of high quality and high integrity. And, of course, Gene Roddenberry thought of himself as somewhat of a modern day Jonathan Swift in that he sought to incorporate meaningful underlying social commentary within all of the *Star Trek* episodes that were produced. So, under the guise of futuristic science fiction, *Star Trek* was able to advance relevant themes regarding race relations and prejudice, war and America's involvement in Vietnam, the role of man versus machine, human sexuality and so many other topics in its weekly telecasts. Again, the appeal of *Star Trek* is apparent as an entertainment form that can be enjoyed by the youngest of audiences as well as those that are seeking a more thought provoking commentary on societal concerns as part of their viewing experience.

Over the years, my passion for *Star Trek* has manifested itself in a desire to collect actual mementos from the production of the series whenever the opportunity arose - subject to affordability and other considerations, of course. The memorabilia that I've collected has not only included various props and costumes that were featured in some of the 79 classic episodes, but has also encompassed other artifacts from the studio such as shooting scripts, filming set concept sketches, Desilu production memos/correspondence on story and script development and, especially, rare behind-the-scenes imagery from the filming of the episodes. My rare image collection, of course, is the source from which the creation of this volume is possible, and it is the subject of a special article in the immediate pages that follow. It has always been particularly thrilling for me to be able to hold something as simple as a little colored resin button in my hand that I know was once part of a control panel on the Desilu Enterprise Bridge filming set; or hold and examine a small film clip that was left over as a remnant of the editing process - discarded to the cutting room floor, if you will - when the studio film editors and technicians were creating the finished master versions of the *Star Trek* episodes. These various artifacts serve as tangible pieces of history that connect one in a powerful and meaningful way, I think, to the creation of a series that many have cherished for decades since childhood. And furthermore, they also serve to connect one to that promising vision for mankind's future that is symbolized by the show.

One can arguably say that *Star Trek* was, or still is, the most successful series in television history. After all, it has spawned a total of no less than 4 subsequent television series and 12 major motion pictures so far; with a 13th film now in production as the Original Series is itself poised to enter its 50th anniversary year soon in 2016. As many have noted, catch-phrases from and references to the show are widespread in today's popular culture; so it should be an exciting time for fans of the franchise to witness how the future of *Star Trek* will unfold in the coming years.

It has been a great thrill for me to work on this volume of rare *Star Trek* images, and I truly hope that some of the photos on these pages bring a smile to your face as you discover them for perhaps the first time, and that you are pleased to add this edition to your personal *Star Trek* library.

Gerald Gurian, October 2015.

Author's Note

The reader should bear in mind that most of the rare imagery which is presented in this volume was captured from a variety of different vintage media sources which included not only small and mid-sized film transparencies, motion picture film and camera negatives but also printed photographs that were originally produced at many different sizes, sometimes quite tiny, in early fanzines and magazines. So the starting resolution and clarity of these rare images, prior to undergoing restoration efforts, was considerably varied.   As a general rule, only the best resolution restored photos were allowed into this volume, with the very rare exception of a small handful that, although of less than perfect quality, were still judged to be of sufficient interest and rarity to warrant their inclusion.

It is also noted that, in general, most of the rare images contained in any episode chapter are presented in chronological sequence based on the filming day that they were taken. This type of arrangement was not possible for every photo , since the date on which some of the pictures were taken is unknown, or other factors may have influenced the presentation sequence.

An Introduction to my Star Trek Rare Image Collection

(Note: Presented below are some selected edited excerpts from an article that was originally published as "A Behind-The-Scenes Look at the Rare Images of Marc Cushman's *These Are The Voyages: TOS - Season One*' and Beyond" on January 4, 2014 at my website *startrekpropauthority.com*.   Some of the original images presented online have been eliminated from this printing due to size and visibility constraints, but the complete article in its original format may still be seen at my website.)

It has been an honor for me to assist my friends Marc Cushman and Susan Osborn with the photo-editing chores for their critically acclaimed book series "These Are The Voyages: TOS ", with the Season One revised edition now in print and the Season Two companion volume coming late next month or early March. Most of the photos presented in the book series are taken from my personal collection of rare *Star Trek* imagery, and so I thought that the readers of this site would enjoy a more detailed look at my collection and some of the restoration work necessary to make the photos appear more presentable.

Many of the rarest TOS images - the clapperboard shots, do not come to us as a result of still photography but are a product of the unused footage shot by the motion picture cameras that were filming the actors performing their scenes for the episodes.

While *Star Trek: The Original Series* was still in production, Gene Roddenberry formed a memorabilia merchandising company called Lincoln Enterprises that sold items such as scripts, postcards, IDIC jewelry, flight deck certificates, tribbles and other collectibles to fans of the show. Among the most distinctive items offered were packets of film clip frames; which contained pieces of the "trims" and "outtakes" (the unused pieces of printed footage) that were left over after the film editors assembled the desirable footage into the finished master versions of the *Star Trek* episodes. Lincoln Enterprises sold different packets of film clips that were sorted based on principal character or other themes. Fans could buy a set containing just footage of Kirk, Spock, McCoy, Uhura or a set featuring aliens, etc. Typically 2 to 3 near identical images were present on each strip of film that varied in length between 1.5" to 2.5". A sample film clip from my collection is shown below - it is a rare behind-the-scenes shot from the 2nd season episode "Who Mourns for Adonais?" (First airdate: Sept. 22, 1967) ...

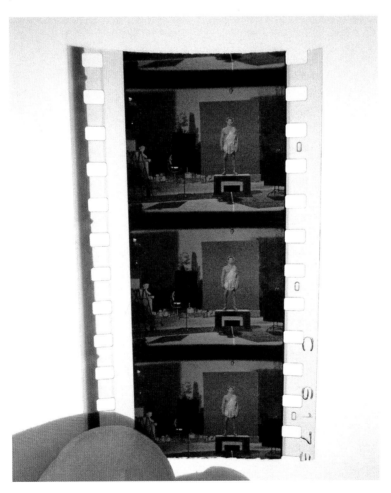

These film clips were advertised in Lincoln's catalogs as being "from the first print "daily" ORIGINALS from the very film that runs through the cameras while they film the show", but technically, that is an incorrect description. The film running through the motion picture cameras would produce a master negative; and these clips are of course positive images - they come from copies that were generated from the master for use by the editing room technicians - and were truly used in the creation of the episodes and collected "from the cutting room floor"!!! Technically, they could not also be called the "dailies" either - since those were the first copies of the filming effort that were generated quickly for viewing by the producers and were always in black and white format - not color. Below is a copy of my Lincoln Enterprises Catalog # 3 that was issued in 1970 and, at right, a close up of the actual ad in the catalog for the Film Clip Frames ...

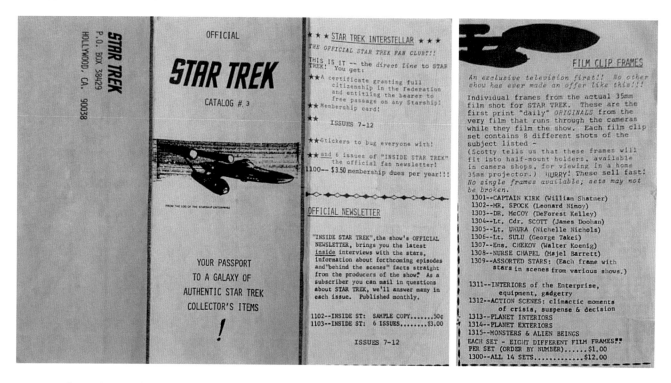

As a youth in the early '70s, I obtained about 700 to 800 of these clips directly from Lincoln, and have steadily grown my collection ever since. As you can see in the catalog, a packet of 8 clips sold for just $1 - or roughly 12 cents per clip.

At present, I own a collection of several thousand individual film cells - but I have deliberately sought out some of the rarest images. For instance, a few years ago I was fortunate to be able to hand-pick several hundred rare images from a rediscovered archive that the folks at Roddenberry.com unearthed which had never been sold by Lincoln.

The vast majority of the Lincoln clips contain ordinary images that appear to be taken from the various scenes that we are familiar with watching as part of the episodes - perhaps they are from an unused take in which an actor failed to say a line correctly or the producer thought should be re-filmed for better effect, and sometimes the actors appear at a slightly different camera angle than we are accustomed to in the final version. However, perhaps every 1 in 100 Lincoln clips contained a rare clapperboard or behind the scenes shot. I have an entire binder in my collection dedicated to just clapperboards. What follows is a sample page from it ...

Even slightly rarer than clapperboard shots are images of the Enterprise and the other starship filming miniatures used in the series. These were frequently distributed by Lincoln as tiny clips with just a single image visible on the film cell - not 2 or 3 identical images.

The following shots present a sampling of my Enterprise film clips. I own some of the smaller size Lincoln clips and dupes, such as those visible at left on the next page, as well as some longer strips showing the 11 foot miniature being filmed at the special effects houses hired by Desilu. For example, the strip that follows at right is a nice shot of the Enterprise on the stage at Film Effects of Hollywood for the production of the 1st season episode "Space Seed" (first airdate: Feb. 16, 1967) ...

I have also segregated out from my general population of film clips those that contain clearly behind-the-scenes imagery but do not feature a clapperboard. These images might show someone from the production crew in the field of view of the camera, or contain a matte painting, a costume test photo or a setup shot for a special effects sequence.

A sampling of some of my images that fall into this category is shown as follows ...

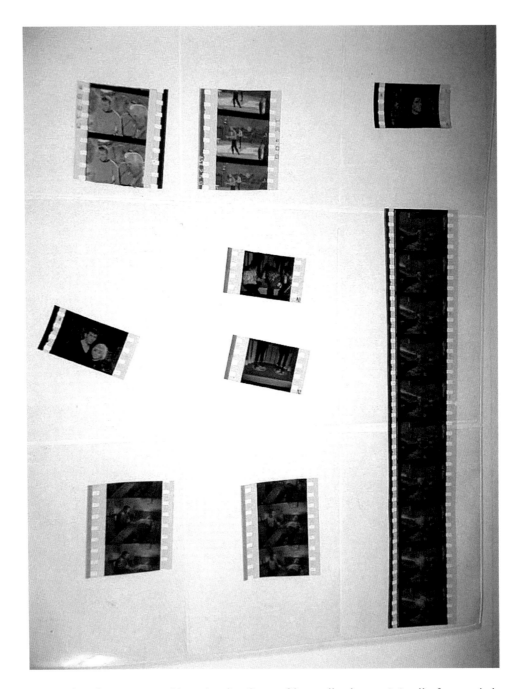

I am also honored to be the owner of hundreds of rare film cells that originally formed the collection of TOS Art Director and Production Designer Walter "Matt" Jefferies - perhaps the one individual most responsible for the look and feel of the various starship sets and the appearance of the alien worlds seen in the original *Star Trek* series. Mr. Jefferies is the creator of the U.S.S. Enterprise starship design, the Klingon battle cruiser design, the interior of the Galileo shuttlecraft, the entire U.S.S. Enterprise bridge layout, and the phaser hand prop - to name just a few.

I believe that he formed the collection, a portion of which is seen at left on the following page, while TOS was being filmed to act as his personal Continuity/Reference album for the various sets and alien worlds that he designed. While this collection does contain more clapperboard shots, there is a pronounced emphasis on grand views of an entire set and frequently the images portray a greater field of vision than was shown in the finished "cropped" view that was incorporated into the broadcast episode.

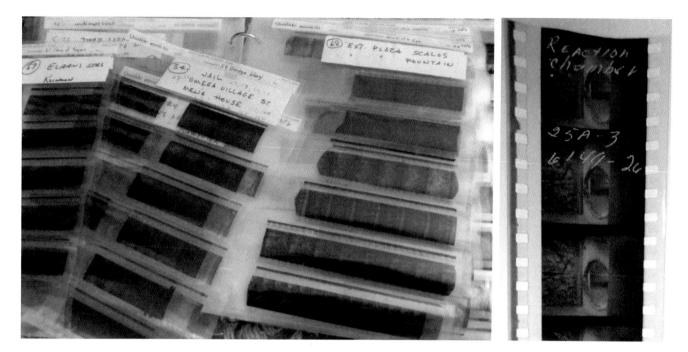

All of these film clips were hand-picked by Matt Jefferies and many contain long pieces of film - of greater size than those typically distributed by Lincoln Enterprises. One can see that most of the pages contain written inscriptions on folded pieces of note paper, executed in Mr. Jefferies hand describing the imagery. Typically, Matt would include the production sequence of the episode on the note and encircle it, at the left hand side of the paper. Imagery from the 2nd season episode "The Omega Glory" (first airdate: Mar. 1, 1968), which was the 54th episode of *Star Trek* that was produced, would thus be identified with a circled number 54 (visible near the center in the above left image.)

At the start of the production of TOS, Matt Jefferies appears to have inscribed some particulars about the imagery directly onto the film strips themselves. For example, the strip visible above at right is from production number 26, the first season episode "The Devil In The Dark" (first airdate: Mar. 9, 1967) .

Some of the most exotic finds within the Jefferies collection include several dozen oversized 2.5" x 2.5" as well as 4" x 5" film photos / transparencies from the production of TOS.

Here is a rare view from the filming of the first TOS pilot, "The Cage". This exciting image, visible in the top left corner of the following page, shows the construction of the set that represents the surface of the planet Talos IV ...

The image seen above at right is a rare 4" x 5" film containing a revealing behind the scenes view of Captain Pike's holding cell in the underground labyrinth on Talos IV.

In addition to my collection of film clips and transparencies, I have also collected rare TOS imagery in the form of printed photos.

Here is a sampling of some of the clapperboard images that I have purchased, below left, and a sampling of some of the vintage TOS publicity photos in my collection, below right, some of which are accompanied by their original Desilu press releases ...

I will not present any photos of the vintage books, magazines, auction catalogs etc. that are also the occasional source of rare TOS imagery - but I can't resist presenting this view, which follows at left, of my collection of a vintage fanzine set called "Inside Star Trek" published in 1968 and 1969 while the show was being filmed. This publication also served as the official newsletter of the show.

I have also been very fortunate to acquire some complete film reels from The Original Series. Shown within the above right image is a vintage reel containing "The Menagerie Pts. 1 and 2" and on top of it in the photo is one of the rare bloopers reels gifted to members of the production crew in late '60s. This bloopers reel consists entirely of rare behind-the-scenes imagery, and I suspect that it, entirely by itself, could be considered the equivalent of thousands of tiny film clips. So far, I have had to utilize it very infrequently during the course of the book project.

So there we have it - an introductory look at some of the elements that make up my Original Series rare image collection. I hope that this does not sound like excessive pride in ownership, but I do believe that my collection represents one of the finest groupings of rare TOS photos in my entire condominium complex.

Now, virtually all of the images included in "These Are The Voyages" have to go through some degree of photo restoration in a photo editing software. In the past 8 months for the first two volumes of the book series, I have literally spent many hundreds of hours engaged in this activity. I am somewhat proficient with the software Corel Paintshop Pro X4 - which I have utilized constantly over the years to fine tune all the imagery that appears on my website.

Here are just a couple of examples from the hundreds of photo restorations that I performed for this book project ...

This is how the original scan appeared of the Enterprise and Botany Bay filming miniatures on the stage at Film Effects of Hollywood for the production of "Space Seed" - the image seen in the long strip of film shown earlier in this article. Notice all the tiny white specks, black spots and blemishes that are spoiling the image throughout ...

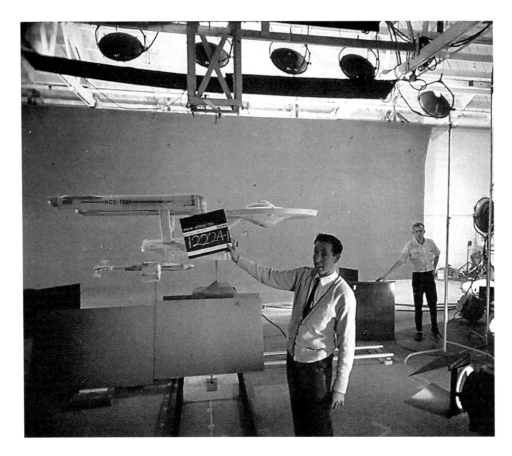

Here is a partially restored color version. Far from perfect, but remember that the goal was to provide a usable black and white copy.

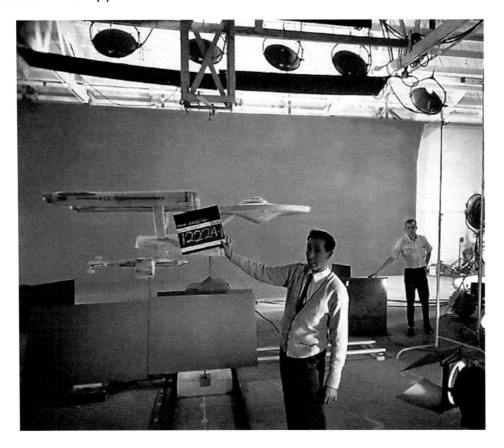

And the final BW version ...

By the way, when I went about transforming a color image into black and white; it wasn't just a matter of choosing a "Convert" function in my photo editing software. It can sometimes be a labor intensive task, as there are many subtle settings that can be manipulated to significantly influence the appearance of the photo - such as brightness, contrast, highlights, midtones, shadows, sharpness and the amount of background noise which might need to be compensated for, and so on, and so on. Tiny blemishes that did not seem distracting at all in the color version can now appear much more pronounced and disconcerting (in need of attention) in the black and white version.

Here is a particularly poor resolution BW image that appeared in Book 1 which was taken from one of the vintage "Inside Star Trek" fanzines seen in an above photo (it was in Issue No. 4, from October 1968). This picture is an extremely rare shot of TOS Prop Master Irving Feinberg and so was considered a highly desirable image for "These Are The Voyages". The original scan appears below at left beside the final BW version at right. Again, not spectacular by any means, but presentable if not enlarged greatly (or shown as a smaller sized image on a printed book page) ...

Many people might not realize that all of the rare images in "These Are The Voyages", because they were never shown as part of an actual '60s TOS television broadcast - were never copyrighted by CBS/Paramount. CBS only has proprietary rights to the footage contained in the broadcast episodes themselves and, in order to have preserved any rights to the rare behind the scenes/clapperboard shots, would have had to literally register each image individually back then according to the copyright laws. Of course, the studio never bothered to expend the time and energy to do so, since no one could have anticipated that unused footage from the show would have any future worth. Who in the world would long remember a supposedly low ratings sci-fi television series that was cancelled after just three seasons? So all of these rare photos have actually fallen into the public domain (according to the Copyright Act of 1976) and may be freely used accordingly.

And now, an embarrassing admission! I hate to say this but I am NOT the most passionate TOS fan in my household! That title would belong to my trusty "pointy eared Science Officer" Minka ...

I have attempted to convince Marc Cushman that the previous image is in fact a rare TOS photo which needs to be included in the book series, or that perhaps it would look nicer on the back cover of the books in place of his own image, but so far he has unwaveringly resisted! (Since Marc has met Minka in person, I'm not extremely confident that he can be convinced the photo dates from the '60s.)

I hope that you have enjoyed this behind the scenes peek into the rare images of "These Are The Voyages: TOS".

Of course, only a small sampling of imagery is contained in this article. To see the complete presentation of rare photos, you would have to consult the books themselves!

Kindest Regards,
Gerald

UPDATE FOR OCTOBER, 2015

In the year and three-quarters since the previous article was first published, I have been fortunate to add not only some new Lincoln clapperboard film cells to my collection, but also quite a few rare 2.25" x 2.25" as well as 35 mm camera negative strips and contact sheets - the byproduct of some still photography on the Desilu soundstages while The Original Series was being filmed ...

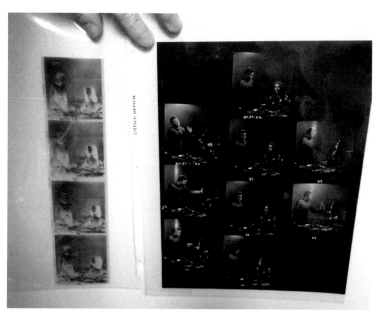

Their presence should only enhance the enjoyment that you might derive in browsing the pages that follow.

Kindest Regards,

Gerald

The Cage

Director: Robert Butler

Writer: Gene Roddenberry

1st Day of Filming: Friday, November 27, 1964   Last Day: Friday, December 18, 1964

Cost: $616,000   16 filming days

Building the Talos IV planet exterior set on the huge Desilu-Culver Stage 16.

The 11 foot 2 inch U.S.S. Enterprise filming miniature, seen outside Volmer Jensen's Burbank, CA Production Models Shop in December, 1964 with (left to right) Vernon Sion, Mel Keys, Volmer Jensen.

A starboard side view of the U.S.S. Enterprise command module, undergoing final scrutiny by Desilu executives and technicians.

The newly constructed Transporter Room set, well stocked with gooseneck viewers.

Leonard Nimoy and Susan Oliver pose for an early makeup test photo.

Model maker Richard Datin presents his newly constructed handiwork, a 3 foot miniature of the U.S.S. Enterprise, to Gene Roddenberry for inspection on location at Desilu 40 Acres.

A dazzling but ultimately unused optical effect for the surface of Talos IV.

Janos Prohaska, who would later portray the iconic Horta and the Mugato on The Original Series, donned a Humanoid Bird costume for the first pilot.

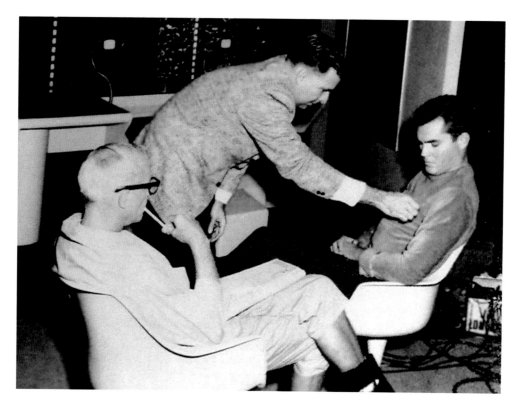

On Day 1 of filming - Friday, November 27, 1964 - Gene Roddenberry ensures Jeffrey Hunter's Starfleet tunic is ready to pass military muster.

Captain On The Bridge! A rare overhead view of the cast on the Bridge set. Note the microphone hanging at upper left, and the electrical wire snaking across the floor by Nimoy's feet.

Captain Pike confronts four Talosians: Jeff Hunter's gaze is presumably towards Director Robert Butler, off set, to receive instructions between takes.

Laurel Goodwin and Majel Barrett on the evening of the second day of filming.

Filming with most of the main cast in the Briefing Room set. Note the soundstage structure above the ceiling is visible.

Principal photography continues at the Helm on Day 5 - Thursday, December 3, 1964.

A servant girl offers food in an unused scene from the Orion Slave Girl dance sequences.

Desilu Exec VP Oscar Katz was notably absent from the soundstage during filming, so the production crew would occasionally send him images like the one above in the hope that he would visit the set.

Unlike Exec VP Katz, Gene Roddenberry maintained a strong presence on the soundstages to actively oversee in the birth of his precious creation. He is seen, above left, reviewing and discussing Meg Wyllie's Talosian make-up with Assistant Director Robert Justman while Peter Duryea looks on; above right, chatting with Duryea during a break in filming; lower left, reviewing some script details with one of the dancers in the Orion trader sequences, and lower right, planning the upcoming picnic scene near Captain Pike's boyhood ranch in Mojave on 23rd century Earth with Susan Oliver, Director Robert Butler and Bob Justman.

Above, a rare image of Costume Designer William Ware Theiss, adjusting the wardrobe of Susan Oliver. Below, a publicity shot of Oliver in the survivors encampment wearing this same outfit.

Susan Oliver in her iconic role as the Green Orion Slave Girl, above, and the human Vina below.

Fred Phillips applies the iconic green body makeup to Susan Oliver while filming the Orion Slave Girl dance sequences on Day 6. When Oliver suddenly became very tired on set, a studio doctor was summoned to administer a vitamin B shot to her. Unfortunately, no one bothered to tell the physician what his patient looked like, and he almost required urgent medical care himself after knocking on Oliver's dressing room door and being confronted with a completely green woman!

Filming at the crash survivors encampment on the surface of Talos IV - aka Stage 16.

Filming the Talosians, Scene 45 Take 2, on Day 9 of production. Meg Wyllie played The Keeper on screen, while the voice work was performed by Malachi Throne. His fee - the cost of a big green velvet wing chair his wife wanted to purchase from Sloan's department store.

Susan Oliver shares a laugh with Hunter and Barrett over a flubbed line while filming on the surface of Talos IV.

Jeff Hunter discusses dialogue with Majel Barrett between takes, while Leonard Nimoy stands with his back to the camera at a Bridge station. Notice the sound microphone visible at upper left.

A rare behind the scenes shot of Albert Whitlock's famous matte painting of the castle on Rigel VII. Note that on three sides of this image, portions of the wood frame surrounding the artwork is visible.

Where No Man Has Gone Before

Director: James Goldstone

Writer: Samuel A. Peeples

1st Day of Filming: Monday, July 19, 1965

Cost: $355,000

Last Day: Thursday, July 29, 1965

9 filming days

William Shatner sits in the Captain's Chair for the first time on Tuesday, July 20, 1965 during Day 2 of filming.

William Shatner between takes with production notes in hand looks off-set, likely, towards Director Goldstone.

Shatner and Andrea Dromm photographed by the turbolift doors at the entry to the Bridge.

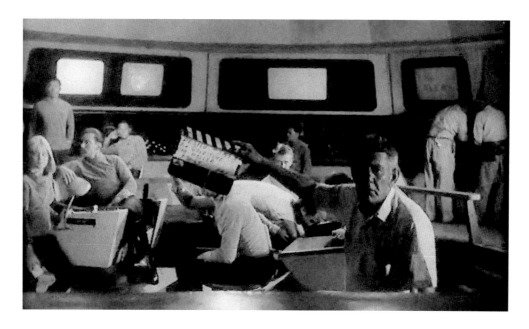

A rare wide angle shot of the principal photography on the Bridge set near the end of production.

James Doohan would join the crew as Chief Engineer Scott for this journey to the edge of the galaxy.

Lloyd Haynes poses for a publicity shot as Communications Officer Lt. Alden. Production Designer Matt Jefferies, who had flown B-17 bombers in WWII and was an aviation enthusiast, was inspired to populate the control panels of Enterprise bridge with actual '50s and '60s aircraft panel buttons.

George Takei would make his debut appearance on *Star Trek* during the filming of the 2nd pilot; wearing what would be an uncharacteristic blue tunic.

Shatner poses with Sally Kellerman in this early publicity shot. The daunting Laser Rifle prop would make its only appearance in this episode. Designed and built for Roddenberry by Reuben Klamer of Toy Development Center, it would fetch an astounding $231,000 when sold at auction by Klamer in April, 2013 during Julien's Hollywood Legends entertainment memorabilia sale. (Image colorized from B&W.)

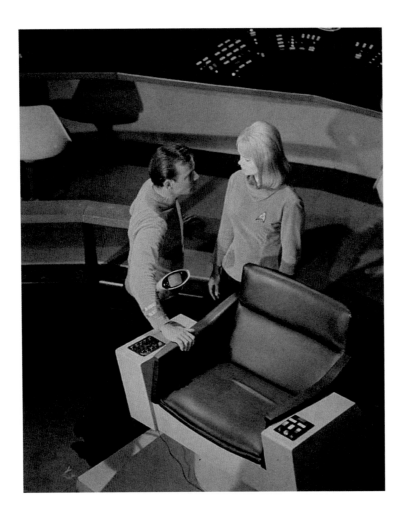

An overhead shot of Shatner chatting with Andrea Dromm by the Captain's Chair

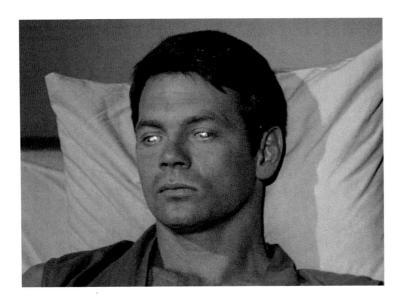

Gary Lockwood wearing his silver contact lenses, in a Lincoln Enterprises film trim. The actor, unlike Sally Kellerman, experienced intense soreness and discomfort while wearing the lenses - which were an old-fashioned "scleral" type that covered the whole eyeball, made especially for the production by John Roberts of Roberts Optical Company. Lockwood would describe filming with them as "the most miserable six days of my life." Beyond discomfort, they also severely limited the actor's vision.

Above left: The new Captain poses for a publicity shot on Day 8 of filming.
Above right: In this NBC publicity photo, Leonard Nimoy leans against the right side of the Bridge Helm and Navigations Console, which has been temporarily relocated to the Transporter Room to serve double duty as the main control station in this important area of the starship.

Filming the 11 foot 2 inch U.S.S. Enterprise miniature on the Howard Anderson Company soundstage on July 23, 1965 for the 2nd pilot.

Wednesday, July 28, 1965 - Day 8 - witnesses Shatner and Lockwood poised to film their climactic encounter on the Exterior Planet set.   Due to delays, the cameras would roll until 9:37pm this night.

William Shatner strikes a pose at a Bridge Station in this early NBC publicity photo.

The Corbomite Maneuver

Director: Joseph Sargent

Writer: Jerry Sohl

1st Day of Filming: Tuesday, May 24, 1966

Last Day: Thursday, June 2, 1966

Cost: $190,430

7 filming days

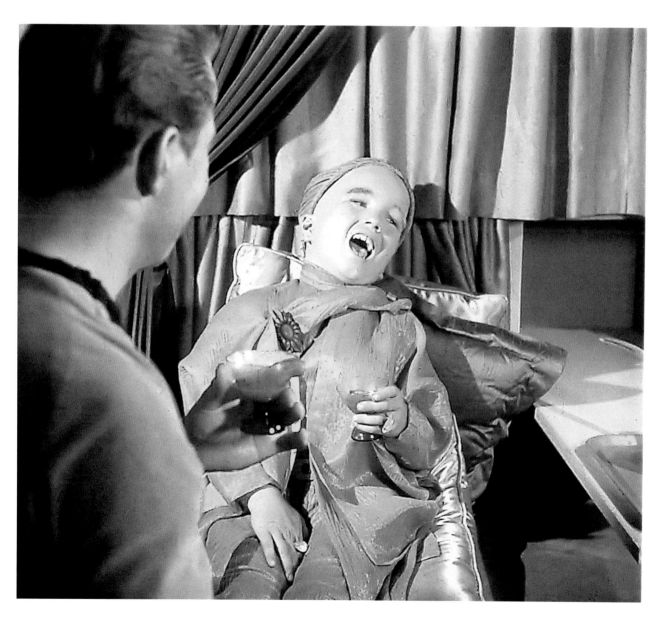

Clint Howard and William Shatner between takes while filming the 1st regular season episode of Season One. Howard, despite an intense dislike for the taste of pink grapefruit juice - aka Tranya - was the consummate professional on screen and appeared to relish its distinct flavor.

A rare view of the filming Bridge set under reconstruction. At far right is SFX Supervisor Jim Rugg.

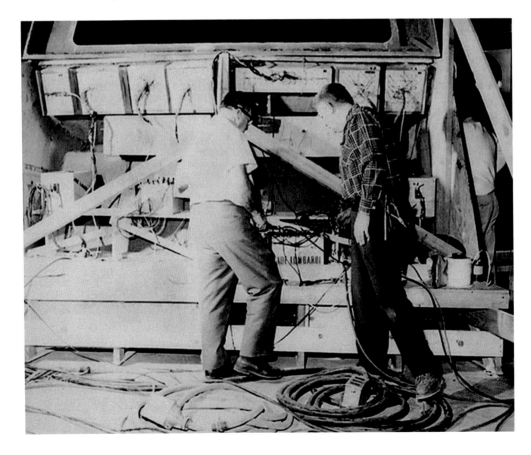

A unique image of Matt Jefferies and Jim Rugg checking cables behind Mr. Spock's Science Station.

In these early NBC publicity shots for the new series, it is apparent that the final costume designs for the 1st season episodes have yet to be realized. William Shatner and Leonard Nimoy are seen in "hybrid" tunics which feature a never-before-seen thick band of black ribbed fabric as the neck collar, while also retaining some soon-to-be obsolete characteristics of the jerseys worn in the pilots: namely, the straight bands of gold rank braid at the wrists which will promptly be substituted with a scalloped edge style, as well as the small 2.25" tall Starfleet insignia patch over the left breast which will be replaced by a more prominent 2.75" high version. Grace Lee Whitney, of course, will undergo the most dramatic change in appearance away from the duty uniforms depicted above, when Gene Roddenberry and company, in acknowledgement of a daring new trend in women's fashion for the 60's, introduced the famous Starfleet miniskirt dress as the standard female attire on the Starship Enterprise. The very first time that Whitney is seen on-screen in an episode of *Star Trek*, she will be wearing her now familiar short red dress; and the only time that she ever wore the older pilot-style female uniform with pants would be the very photoshoot that created the above pair of publicity photos along with a small handful of similar pictures.

Still outfitted in his "hybrid" part-pilot, part-regular season tunic, Nimoy poses for an early publicity shot with the 3 foot U.S.S. Enterprise filming miniature.

The temperamental guest star - the creation of Wah Chang - demands a cigarette break!

Associate Producer John D. F. Black chats with a friend during production.

Grace Lee Whitney in a deleted scene from the Captain's Quarters.

George Takei and Anthony Call man the sophisticated U.S.S. Enterprise helm.

Shatner reviews some last minute dialogue changes with his co-star. (Image colorized from B&W.)

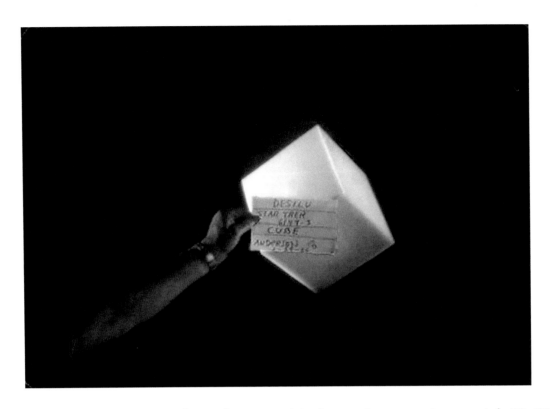

Filming the mysterious alien cube at the Howard Anderson Company stage on July 12, 1966.

A wide view of the bridge set during production. Note Nichelle Nichols is wearing a gold command dress in this episode, and the ceiling of the set - with studio lights and sound equipment - is visible.

Shatner and Kelley plan an impending scene on the First Federation vessel.

Leonard Nimoy is slated for a bridge shot on Friday, May 27, 1966 - Day 4 of production.

Nichelle Nichols relaxes in the Briefing Room between takes on Day 6.

Anthony Call and DeForest Kelley share a moment of levity on set.

Captain Kirk poses with the menacing alter-ego of the Captain of the Fesarius.

Mudd's Women

Director: Harvey Hart

Writer: Stephen Kandel

1st Day of Filming: Thursday, June 2, 1966   Last Day: Monday, June 13, 1966

Cost: $198,534   8 filming days

Shatner and Nimoy pose in the Transporter alcove for a publicity shot with (from left) Maggie Thrett, Susan Denberg and Karen Steele. (Image colorized from B&W.)

Not including the recurring regular cast and Enterprise crewmen, Roger C. Carmel would be the only guest star on The Original Series to portray the same character in more than one episode when he reprised his role of Harry Mudd in the 2nd season for "I, Mudd". In the Briefing Room image, above, the post production team has yet to include a graphic display on the computer monitor.

Shatner, Nimoy and Doohan on Friday, June 3rd - Day 2 of production.

Commander Spock has the Con! As filming proceeds on the second day.

Karen Steele on Day 6 of production, as Eve, withdrawing from the effects of the Venus drugs.

Nimoy with Thrett.

Nimoy with Denberg.

Filming with a futuristic set of round cards on Day 7. The cards were actually a commercially available, off-the-shelf product sold as Ace Round Playing Cards as well as the Jajaco brand.

A view of the miner's enclosed encampment on the hostile surface of Rigel XII on Day 8.

Gene Roddenberry could not allow the production to complete without availing himself of the opportunity to pose with his three lovely guest stars.

The Enemy Within

Director: Leo Penn

Writer: Richard Matheson

1st Day of Filming: Tuesday, June 14, 1966   Last Day: Wednesday, June 22, 1966

Cost: $193,646   7 filming days

William Shatner and his body double, Don Eitner, prepare to film in the Transporter Room set, with Nimoy and Kelley.

Filming on the surface of Alfa 177 - aka Stage 10 - on Day 1 of production.

Slating the shot on Wednesday, June 15, 1966 - Day 2.

James Doohan is slated for a close up of Scotty operating the Transporter on Day 2. This footage, which has been designated as "Stock-FX", is of such a generic nature that it could easily be reused in future episodes whenever a landing party is beamed to/from a planet's surface.

A moment of levity between William Shatner and Grace Lee Whitney as they film what would be a daring and controversial scene for '60s television - the first attempted rape shown on NBC.

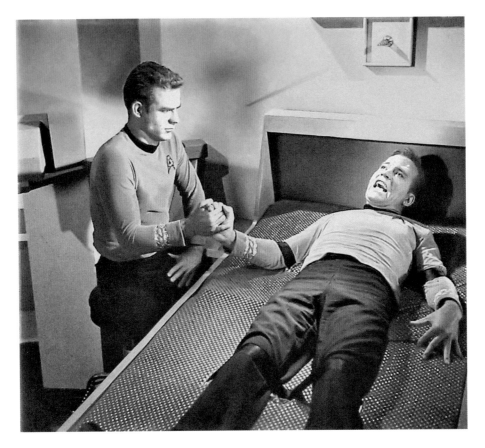

Shatner and Eitner reverse positions during the complex split-screen filming process employed to capture the memorable Sickbay interaction between the "good" Kirk and the "evil" Kirk.

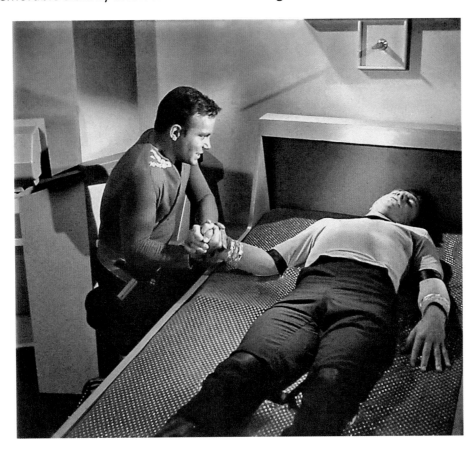

Production resumes on the Bridge on Day 4 with Shatner, Nimoy and Kelley.

DeForest Kelley and William Shatner in Sickbay on Day 6.

The beautiful Grace Lee Whitney is captured in some playful candid moments on set: posing with Leonard Nimoy, above, and in the Briefing Room set below. (Bottom image colorized from B&W.)

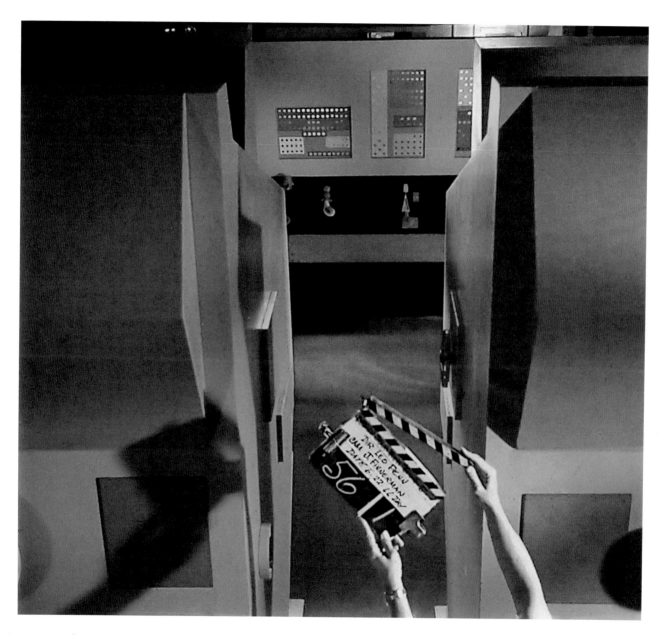

An unusual camera angle peering into Main Engineering is slated on Wednesday, June 22, 1966 - Day 7 and the final day of production.

An NBC publicity photo for the dramatic attempted rape scene.

The Man Trap

Director: Marc Daniels

Writer: George Clayton Johnson

1st Day of Filming: Wednesday, June 22, 1966

Cost: $185,401

Last Day: Thursday, June 30, 1966

7 filming days

Captain Kirk and the M-113 creature in an NBC publicity photo

Filming the climactic attack on the Captain - on Friday, June 24, 1966 - Day 3 of production.

Director Marc Daniels with William Shatner and Jeanne Bal on Day 3.

Dancer and actress Sharon Gimpel was the talent inside the M-113 Salt Vampire costume - it would be her sole Hollywood screen performance.

Bill McGovern slates a shot on Stage 10 amidst the ancient ruins on the planet M-113. This impressive temple was in reality constructed of cardboard boxes sprayed with gummite.

Filming proceeds in the Briefing Room on Monday, June 27, 1966 - Day 4.

A make-up test shot featuring Frank Da Vinci shows the after-effects of a Salt Vampire attack.

Slating a shot on the 6th day of production - with more carnage caused by this creature!

Some additional views of Director Daniels and cast planning the Salt Vampire death scenes.

In the above Bridge set behind-the-scenes image, note at top center how a special overhead floodlight has been positioned to better illuminate the actors in the scene. Also, because of the distance separating the cast, two overhead microphones are employed for proper sound capture.

Jeanne Bal poses with the M-113 creature's delicacy - salt - in this NBC publicity shot.

While "The Man Trap" was the very first episode of *Star Trek* to be broadcast on network television, with an original airdate of September 8, 1966, it was actually the 4th regular season episode of the series to be produced, not counting the 2nd pilot "Where No Man Has Gone Before" which was of course filmed in July, 1965 and used to sell the show to NBC. "The Man Trap" was the first time that Nichelle Nichols would be seen wearing her now familiar red miniskirt Starfleet duty uniform; as she was previously filmed in a gold colored command division dress. In this early publicity photo, the image of Nichols has been surprisingly superimposed over a scene from the first pilot "The Cage" - a production in which she did not make an appearance.

The Naked Time

Director: Marc Daniels

Writer: John D. F. Black

1st Day of Filming: Thursday, June 30, 1966

Last Day: Monday, July 11, 1966

Cost: $174,269

7 filming days

Filming in the frozen laboratory on planet Psi 2000 on Friday July 1, 1966 - Day 2 of production.

Beware the Swashbuckling Helmsman! According to his recollections in his book "Star Trek Memories" (1993, Harper Collins), William Shatner claims he was in genuine fear of injury at the hands of his over-zealous co-star, George Takei, who took to his role as master swordsman with unbridled passion. Meanwhile, apparently, Leonard Nimoy was cracking up with laughter every time Shatner yelped out in pain.

Director Marc Daniels does his utmost to bring out the finest from his talent - in this case, actor Bruce Hyde, who would give an unforgettable performance as Lt. Kevin Riley.

Nimoy poses for an NBC publicity shot on Day 2 with a department store mannequin.

William Shatner and James Doohan share a laugh on Friday, July 8, 1966 - Day 6 of production. In this screenshot from the famous blooper reels, Shatner is pleading "Somebody help the Captain!"

More of the dashing d'Artagnan of the Enterprise. And yes, the door behind George Takei was indeed colored yellow in this image, when it was released by the studio as a 5" x 7" postcard.

The beautiful Nichelle Nichols allows her playful spirit to grace the camera with many artistic poses that were captured during an impromptu photo session on the Desilu soundstages.

Nichols assumes a particularly striking pose. Between the ages of 12 and 14, she had studied classical ballet at the Chicago Ballet Academy; and she began her career as a singer and dancer.

William Shatner finally turns the tables on George Takei in this posed publicity shot.

Charlie X

Director: Lawrence Dobkin

Writer: D. C. Fontana

1st Day of Filming: Monday, July 11, 1966

Last Day: Tuesday, July 19, 1966

Cost: $177,941

7 filming days

Robert Walker Jr. and Grace Lee Whitney in an NBC publicity photo

Shatner and Walker prepare to film in the gymnasium, to teach Charlie the art of self defense.

Nimoy, Shatner and Whitney plan an upcoming take.

Slating a scene with Robert Walker Jr. on Friday, July 15, 1966 - Day 5 of production.

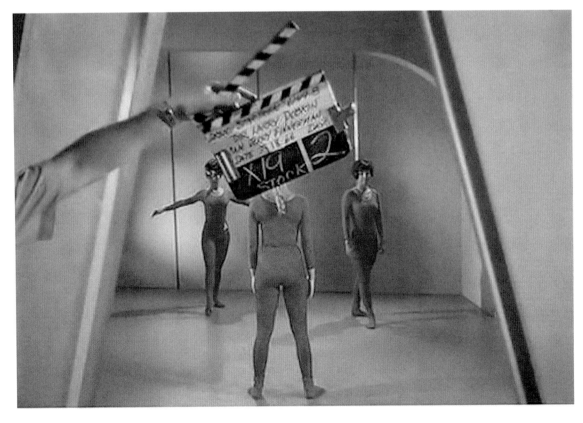

A rare look at the female Starfleet workout attire - perhaps the inspiration for later series catsuits.

On Day 6, July 18th, Shatner and Walker performed the wrestling scenes with the Captain fully clothed as well as shirtless. Despite William Shatner's expressed preference to keep his robe on, Desilu Exec Herb Solow in consultation with Gene Roddenberry overruled the series star and filming proceeded with Kirk topless, as it was felt that was what the viewing audience would want to see.

Balance of Terror

Director: Vincent McEveety

Writer: Paul Schneider

1st Day of Filming: Wednesday, July 20, 1966   Last Day: Thursday, July 28, 1966

Cost: $236,150   7 filming days

Barry Mason slates a shot of the Romulan Bird-of-Prey on the Film Effects of Hollywood soundstage.

Bill McGovern slates a scene with Paul Comi as Lt. Stiles on the Bridge on Day 2 of production.

Stephen Mines as Lt. Robert Tomlinson, the only Starfleet casualty in this encounter with the Romulans - on what was intended to be his wedding day.

Mark Lenard, who would later play the role of Sarek, Spock's father, in "Journey to Babel" and three feature films as well as in episodes of *Star Trek: TNG*, made his *Original Series* debut in this episode as the Romulan Commander.   He is seen above in a deleted scene, nodding in acknowledgement to Captain Kirk immediately before triggering the self-destruct mechanism on his ship.

Gary Walberg, the Commander of the ill-fated Outpost 4, in a Lincoln film trim.

Filming on the Romulan Bridge on Wednesday, July 27, 1966 - Day 6 of production.

Some additional images of the Bird-of-Prey miniature on the shooting stage at Film Effects. In the top photo, at left, one of the three owners of the company, Don Weed, supports the model by its nacelle.

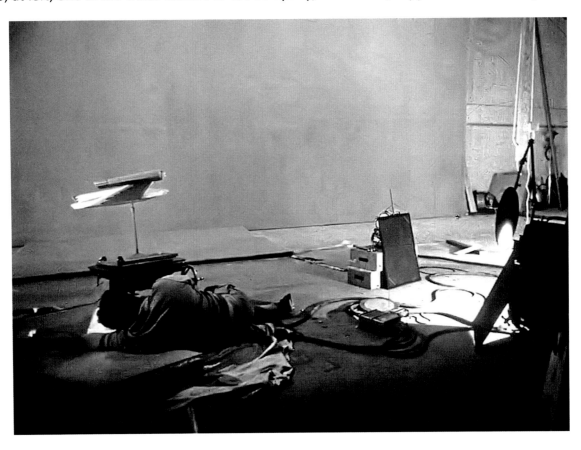

What Are Little Girls Made Of?

Director: James Goldstone

Writer: Robert Bloch

1st Day of Filming: Thursday, July 28, 1966

Last Day: Tuesday, August 9, 1966

Cost: $211,061

9 filming days

William Shatner and Sherry Jackson dancing atop the Android Duplicator in the underground chambers of the planet Exo III - aka Stage 10. Note that Shatner has dispensed with his Starfleet boots in favor of a more comfortable pair of penny loafers.

Slating a scene in the underground caverns with Shatner and Majel Barrett on Day 2 of production.

William Shatner and his body double in the process of filming the split-screen effect in Korby's study.

The lovely Sherry Jackson graciously models her android jumpsuit for the camera.

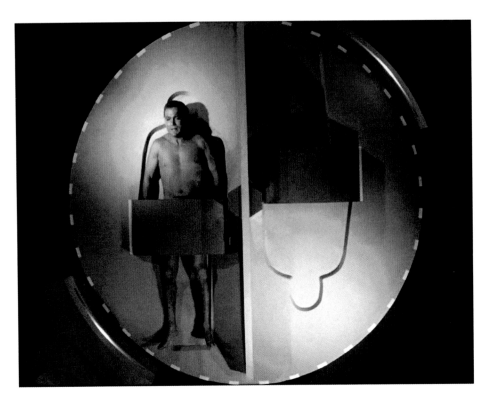

A special effects shot, prior to the duplication of Shatner's image on the other side of the turntable.

William Shatner and Majel Barrett pose for a publicity shot in the ruins of Exo III.

Sherry Jackson and William Shatner in an NBC publicity photo. (Image colorized from B&W.)

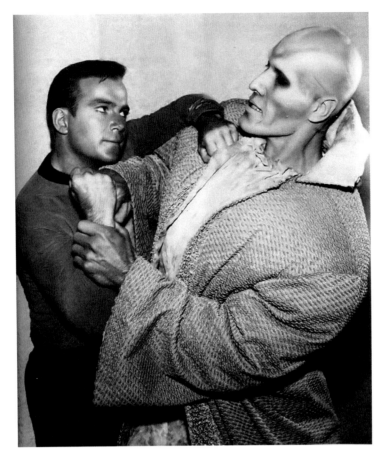

Above: An official publicity shot of the Captain and Ruk. Below: A less-than-official version.

Ted Cassidy and William Shatner clowning around again as production continues on Stage 10.

It was during the filming of this episode that one of the most famous production crew pranks took place, at the expense of Leonard Nimoy. As Nimoy was preparing to film a scene in the Captain's Chair, his 10 year old son Adam - fully adorned with a set of pointed Vulcan Ear makeup appliances, just like those worn by his father - made an unannounced entrance onto the Bridge through the Turbolift doors, walked straight up to his father, kissed him on the cheek and said "Hi, Daddy!" to the surprised amusement of the senior Nimoy. Adam was a frequent visitor to the *Star Trek* sets while the series was in production, also witnessing the filming of different scenes from such episodes as "The Man Trap", "Operation: Annihilate!" and "The Trouble With Tribbles". Below, he is seen assisting make-up man Fred Phillips with the transformation of his dad into the legendary First Officer of the U.S.S. Enterprise.

Dagger of the Mind

Director: Vincent McEveety

Writer: Shimon Wincelberg (as S. Bar-David)

1st Day of Filming: Tuesday, August 9, 1966

Last Day: Wednesday, August 17, 1966

Cost: $182,140

7 filming days

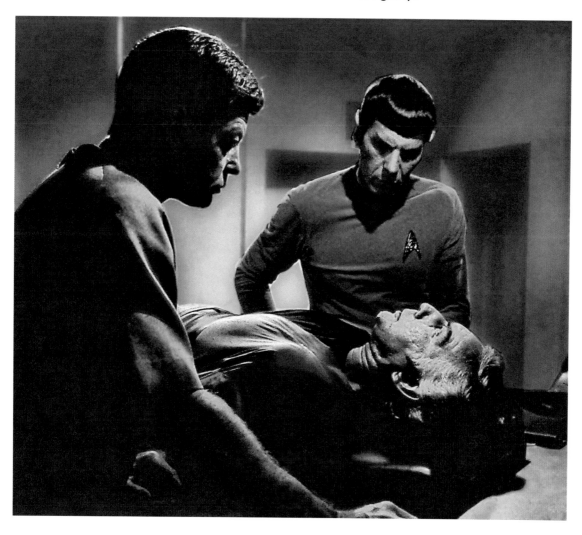

Morgan Woodward with DeForest Kelley and Leonard Nimoy in Sickbay in an unaired Lincoln film trim. Woodward would reflect that his portrayal of Simon Van Gelder, with all of the intense outpouring of emotion involved, was the most difficult role that he would ever play.

Marianna Hill in her role as Dr. Helen Noel in an NBC publicity photo.

Leonard Nimoy in a deleted scene in the Neural Neutralizer Room of the Tantalus Penal Colony.

Marianna Hill poses with Editor Bruce Schoengarth in this behind-the-scenes image.

Slating a shot with Marianna Hill on Monday, August 15, 1966 - Day 5 of production.

Production continues on Day 6 in a scene with James Gregory, Hill and Shatner.

William Shatner between takes in the "treatment" chair.

Miri

Director: Vincent McEveety

Writer: Adrian Spies

1st Day of Filming: Monday, August 22, 1966   Last Day: Tuesday, August 30, 1966

Cost: $206,815   7 filming days

Shatner and company film at the huge Desilu 40 Acres lot in Culver City, California.   This particular set of city streets, which was employed in the episode to represent the abandoned city on the strange Earth-like planet populated by the "Onlies" children; was famous for being the town of Mayberry in The Andy Griffith Show.   Note Bill McGovern at lower right with slate in hand.

Kim Darby and William Shatner in an NBC publicity photo.

Slating a shot with Kim Darby in the title role as Miri.

Shatner, Whitney, Kelley and Darby film in the makeshift research lab on Day 2 of production.

Between takes on the streets of Mayberry.

Ed McCready, Leonard Nimoy and William Shatner in an NBC publicity photo.

Filming in the town square on Wednesday, August 24, 1966 - Day 3.

Bill McGovern slates a shot on Day 7, the final day of production, with some Onlies children. The young lady at center is Darleen Roddenberry - who along with her sister Dawn were brought in to the studio by their father to participate in this episode. William Shatner's daughters Leslie and Lisabeth, as well as Grace Lee Whitney's sons Jonathan and Scott also appeared on screen in this show.

The Conscience of the King

Director: Gerd Oswald

Writer: Barry Trivers

1st Day of Filming: Tuesday, September 13, 1966

Last Day: Wednesday, September 21, 1966

Cost: $184,859

7 filming days

Arnold Moss and Barbara Anderson in an NBC publicity photo.

Shatner and Anderson gaze off set, presumably towards Director Oswald, for input between takes.

In this deleted scene, the crew watches the Shakespearean performance broadcast on the monitor.

Some rare shots of the cast and crew were captured by a team from Ebony magazine, which visited the set during the filming of this episode in order to prepare for an upcoming article on Nichelle Nichols - which would be prominently featured in the January 1967 issue of the publication. Above, Nimoy and Nichols pose for the camera; while below, Nichols chats with DeForest Kelley as Costume Designer Bill Theiss measures her for a new set of Starfleet boots.

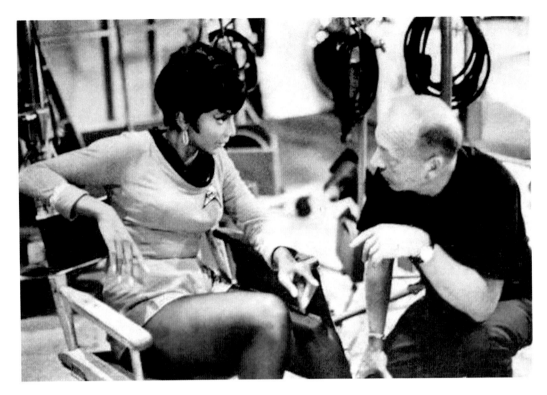

Some additional behind-the-scenes imagery captured by Ebony magazine staff: Nichelle Nichols receives last-minute instructions from Director Gerd Oswald between takes, above, and serenades fellow actors Frank Vince and Ron Veto with the Vulcan Lyre prop that Uhura will play onscreen for Lt. Kevin Riley, below left. In the bottom right photo, Nichols is seen reviewing her script while simultaneously receiving a minor costume adjustment from wardrobe mistress Maggie Makau and a hair style touchup from makeup artist Virgina Darcey.

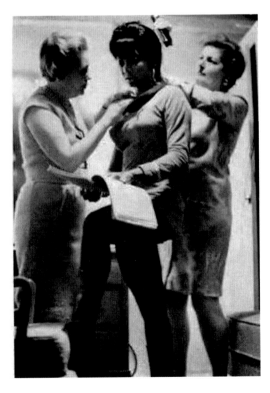

Moss and Anderson in an official publicity shot.

Nimoy and Kelley crack up after missing their lines during filming in the Captain's Quarters.

Bill McGovern slates a shot on the Observation Deck of the U.S.S. Enterprise.

Shatner and Anderson between takes on the Observation Deck.

A final candid image of Nichelle Nichols captures the actress as she rides her studio bicycle between buildings on the Desilu lot.

The Galileo Seven

Director: Robert Gist

Writer: Oliver Crawford and Shimon Wincelberg (as S. Bar-David)

1st Day of Filming: Thursday, September 22, 1966   Last Day: Friday, September 30, 1966

Cost: $232,690   7 filming days

Leonard Nimoy poses by the Shuttlecraft Galileo in an NBC publicity shot. (Image colorized from B&W.)

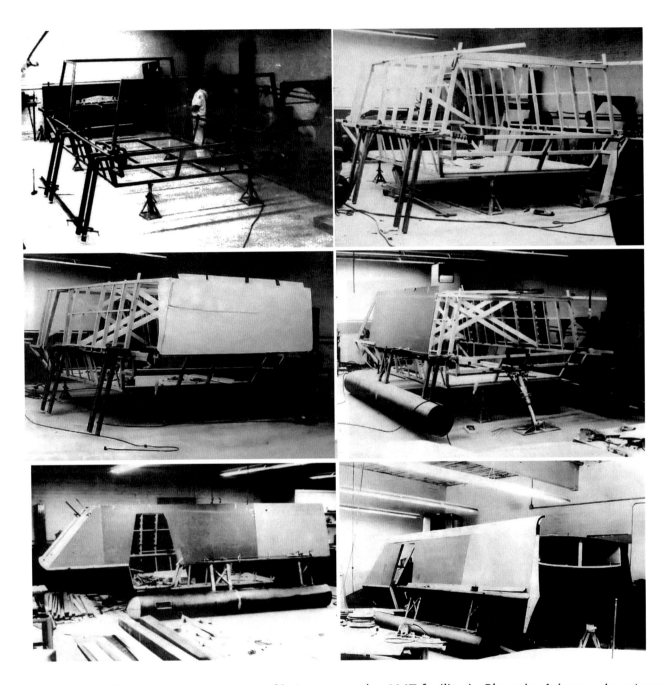

Building the Galileo shuttlecraft exterior filming set at the AMT facility in Phoenix, Arizona. In return for absorbing all of the costs associated with constructing and delivering the Galileo sets (interior and exterior), as well as providing a 3' shuttlecraft filming miniature; AMT acquired the exclusive rights to produce and market the starship Enterprise model kits. The total costs, fully paid by AMT, came out to be $24,000 and the various sets were delivered to Desilu on September 12, 1966 - a full 10 days ahead of the start of filming. The exterior filming set was built to 3/4 scale, and its interior floor to ceiling height measured just 5 feet, so an actor could not stand fully upright when inside it. The interior filming set, which included the detailed cockpit and passenger areas, was built full size.

Some rare shots of the Galileo exterior set on the surface of the planet Taurus II - aka Stage 10. Note the rafters in the ceiling of the soundstage are just barely discernible at top left in the above photo.

A view of the cockpit of the Galileo shuttlecraft interior filming set. The interior was designed by Matt Jefferies, while celebrated custom car designer Gene Winfield created the shuttlecraft exterior.

This image from a deleted scene shows the shuttlecraft withstanding the heat of atmospheric entry.

Filming the 3' long shuttlecraft miniature on the Film Effects of Hollywood stage. It was shot inside a 10' long by 6' wide model of the U.S.S. Enterprise Hanger Bay built by Richard Datin for this episode.

This image features the 3' Galileo filming miniature seen against a projected star field.

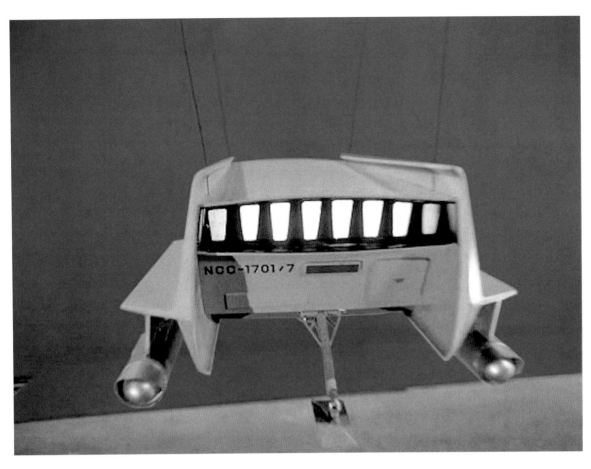

Some additional views of the 3' shuttlecraft model on the Film Effects stage, against a blue screen.

Robert "Big Buck" Maffei, at 7' 1" in height, was cast as the Taurus II humanoid. He is seen here slated from an unused camera angle. Note the top of the set visible in the upper left corner.

The publicity shot of Buck Maffei in costume at left was deemed too gruesome by NBC for public release. It was replaced with the one of Nimoy at right.

Stage lights positioned above help illuminate the Galileo crew seen inside the full scale shuttlecraft interior filming set on Day 6 of production.

A unique camera angle of the Bridge from above, as specified by Director Robert Gist.

Buck Maffei and Phyllis Douglas between takes.

Shuttlecraft designer Gene Winfield poses beside his creation with Leonard Nimoy.

Court Martial

Director: Marc Daniels

Writer: Dan Mankiewicz and Steven W. Carabatsos

1st Day of Filming: Monday, October 3, 1966

Last Day: Tuesday, October 11, 1966

Cost: $175,182

7 filming days

Bill McGovern slates the shot as the trial resumes on the Bridge of the U.S.S. Enterprise.

Above left, filming proceeds on Day 1 with a close-up view of the courtroom computer as witness testimony is about to begin. Above right, Joan Marshall as Lt. Areel Shaw is slated for a shot on Friday October 7, 1966 - Day 5 of production.

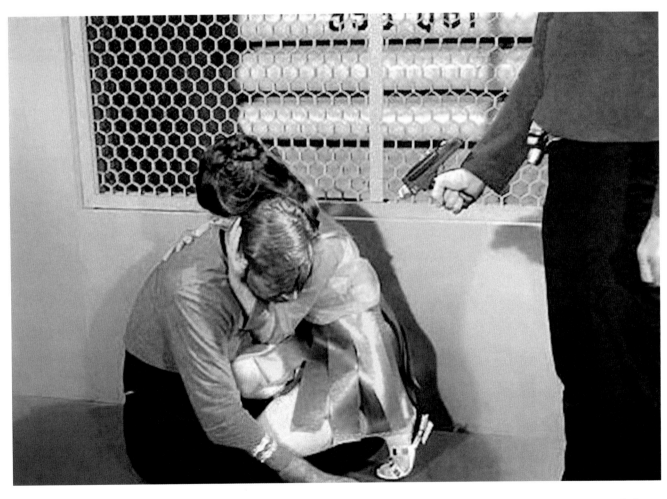

In this deleted scene image, Jame Finney comforts her father in engineering while security stands by.

From a blooper reel, Elisha Cook flubs a line - apparently a fairly common occurrence on this set.

On Day 7 - October 11, 1966 - Elisha Cook and William Shatner continue filming in the courtroom with, hopefully, a minimal number of dialogue errors.

William Shatner can be seen breaking out in a faint smile, at bottom center, as Director Marc Daniels addresses the cast between takes while filming in the courtroom.

The Menagerie, Pts 1 & 2

Director: Marc Daniels

Writer: Gene Roddenberry

1st Day of Filming: Tuesday, October 11, 1966

Last Day: Tuesday, October 18, 1966

Cost: $220,953

6 filming days

Leonard Nimoy, William Shatner and Malachi Throne film portions of Mr. Spock's court martial trial in this unaired Lincoln film trim.

Above, the Starbase 11 beam down site was little more than a physical wall and some accompanying statuary as constructed on Desilu's Stage 10. Below, it's final on-screen appearance when composited into footage that included Al Whitlock's futuristic matte painting as a background.

Malachi Throne as Commodore Jose Mendez in a moment of levity between takes.

A special effects composite shot featuring footage from "The Cage".

Slating a shot with Malachi Throne in the Transporter Room on Day 2 of filming.

Sean Kenney in his elaborate, disfigured Captain Pike makeup on Thursday, October 13, 1966 - Day 3.

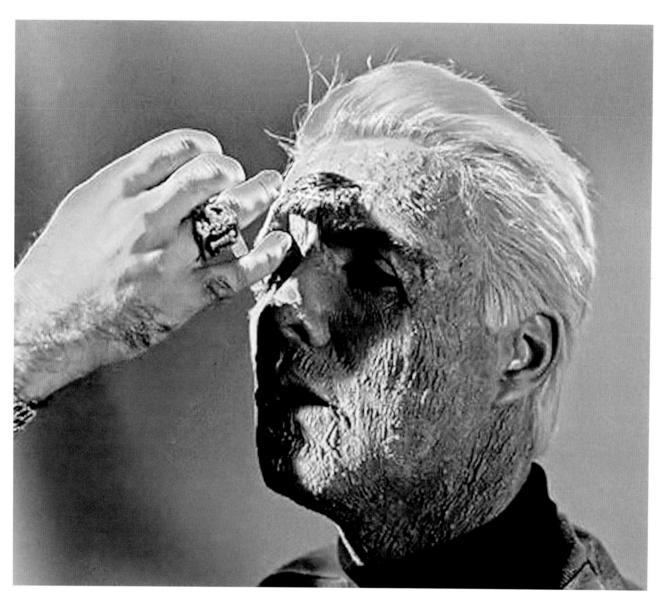

Sean Kenney gets a touch-up to his elaborate make-up between takes. Kenney was only 22 years old when cast to portray the aged and injured former Captain of the Enterprise.

Shore Leave

Director: Robert Sparr

Writer: Theodore Sturgeon

1st Day of Filming: Wednesday, October 19, 1966

Last Day: Thursday, October 27, 1966

Cost: $199,654

7 filming days

George Takei inspects the Black Knight automaton as filming proceeds at Africa USA on Day 2.

Emily Banks as Yeoman Tonia Barrows and DeForest Kelley on location at Africa USA.

Bill McGovern slates a shot as Shatner and Nimoy observe the Black Knight from afar.

The Black Knight in the midst of his charge as captured in an NBC publicity shot.

Bruce Mars in a Lincoln film trim of his unforgettable portrayal of upperclassman Finnegan.

Bill Shatner in an unaired Lincoln trim during Kirk's fight sequence with Finnegan.

Above left, DeForest Kelley is slated for a close up shot on Day 5 of production. Above right, Shatner in torn shirt and Nimoy are slated for the scene that follows the Kirk Finnegan skirmish.

William Shatner and Leonard Nimoy rehearse dialogue between takes on Day 6 while on location at Africa USA. With temperatures dropping as the filming day stretched into the evening hours, Nimoy wears a blanket for warmth.

The Squire of Gothos

Director: Don McDougall

Writer: Paul Schneider

1st Day of Filming: Friday, October 28, 1966   Last Day: Monday, November 7, 1966

Cost: $194,573   7 filming days

William Campbell as "General" Trelane, Retired in an NBC publicity photo.

Actress Venita Wolf, as Yeoman Teresa Ross, is seen with William Shatner between takes.

Day 4: An M-113 creature, or Salt Vampire, as seen in "The Man Trap" on display in Trelane's castle.

Shatner, Campbell and Nichols discuss an upcoming scene between takes.

Cinematographer Jerry Finnerman, whose brilliant use of colored lights created the many stunning alien skyscapes seen in TOS, and the artistic lightning of so many sets aboard ship, skillfully projected a surreal noose on the wall behind William Shatner in this shot to provide an added dramatic effect.

Bill Campbell prepares to give chase to Shatner in the woods outside the castle on Day 7.

Let the hunt begin! Scene 97B Take 1

Venita Wolf and William Shatner together again in an NBC publicity shot.

Arena

Director: Joseph Pevney

Writer: Gene L. Coon

1st Day of Filming: Tuesday, November 8, 1966   Last Day: Tuesday, November 15, 1966

Cost: $197,586   6 filming days

Bobby Clark as the Gorn on location at Vasquez Rocks on November 10, 1966 - Day 3 of production.

Pieces of the iconic Gorn costume on display in the backyard of Wah Chang's home, where it was created inside a work shed behind the house. Note the silver eyes have yet to be completed.

Another view of the costume under construction at the home of Wah Chang. The foundation of the design was a soft rubber wetsuit, onto which layers of sculpted foam muscles and reptilian details were affixed. In the photo above, the lower half - still unpainted - is being modeled.

A rare view of Bobby Clark without the Gorn head, which is being held by a member of the costume department. Note the black makeup around Clark's lower face.

William Shatner and Bobby Clark discuss the filming of the upcoming fight sequence between takes. (Image colorized from B&W.)

An unaired Lincoln film trim from the historic battle between the two Starship Captains!

In this behind-the-scenes photo, note that a pair of ventilation holes in the lower half of the Gorn costume are visible just below the multi-colored tunic. Not only did the costume build up tremendously uncomfortable levels of heat while being worn, but the legs were permanently affixed in a standing position and so the actor inside could not even sit down while resting between takes.

Above left: Preparing to film a close up view of Leonard Nimoy peering through the Library Computer Station viewfinder at Mr. Spock's Science station on the Bridge on Day 1 of production. Above right: Slating a shot on location at Vasquez Rocks, with a Gorn visible through the legs, on Day 2.

Filming on Day 4 in the fort at Vasquez Rocks - aka the Federation outpost on Cestus III.

Some rare behind-the-scenes still photos of the cast and crew taken by actor Eddie Paskey aka Lt. Leslie, who decided to bring his camera along for the days filming on location in the fort at Vasquez Rocks. Shatner and Nimoy appear with scripts in hand in the top photos, while Kelley faces the camera and a pyrotechnic effect is set off in the images below.

Heading out for a night on the town! Both Bobby Clark and Gary Combs would don the Gorn costume during production to portray this famous *Star Trek* alien.

Bobby Clark strikes a magnificent pose between takes in this behind-the-scenes photo.

The Alternative Factor

Director: Gerd Oswald

Writer: Don Ingalls

1st Day of Filming: Wednesday, November 16, 1966   Last Day: Friday, November 25, 1966

Cost: $210,879   7 filming days

William Shatner and Robert Brown in an NBC publicity photo.

Leonard Nimoy with script on location during filming at Vasquez Rocks.

Director Gerd Oswald and Leonard Nimoy between takes while on location.

Slating a scene with Shatner at Vasquez Rocks on Tuesday, November 22, 1966 - Day 5 of production.

Shatner stands in the "negative magnetic corridor" between the two parallel universes, aka Stage 10. The post production team has yet to add the shimmering and negative imagery to this shot.

Shatner freezes in position in this pre-special effects shot in Lazarus's spaceship.

An unused special effects shot of Lazarus's vehicle taking phaser fire from the Enterprise.

Preparing to film the two Lazaruses struggling for eternity in the magnetic corridor on Day 7.

The struggling will commence between these unrelenting combatants at any moment!

Tomorrow Is Yesterday

Director: Michael O'Herlihy

Writer: D.C. Fontana

1st Day of Filming: Monday, November 28, 1966   Last Day: Monday, December 5, 1966

Cost: $178,629   6 filming days

George Takei and William Shatner share a laugh over a missed line while filming in the "Statistical Services Division 498th Airbase Group" offices at the US Air Force base in Earth's past, aka Stage 10.

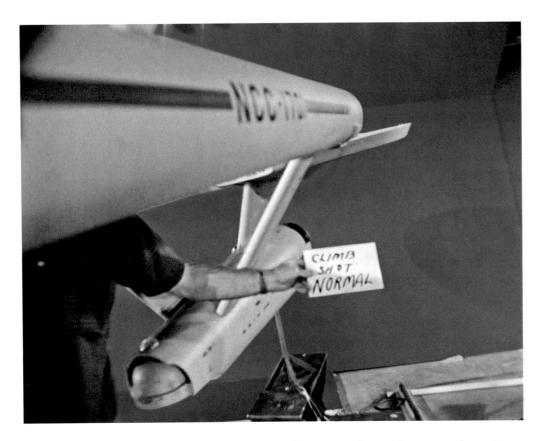

Ultimately unused footage of the U.S.S. Enterprise climbing out of Earth's atmosphere is captured on the Howard Anderson Co. soundstage.

While the Enterprise soars through Earth's skies in this NBC publicity photo.

Above left, from a blooper reel, a moment of levity while filming Kirk's interrogation scenes at the air base. Above right, a Lincoln film trim featuring Roger Perry as Captain Christopher on the Enterprise turbolift.

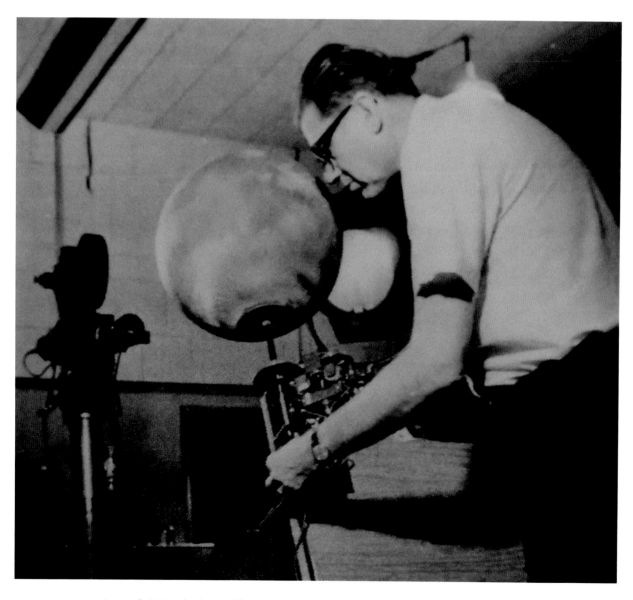

Joseph Westheimer films a rotating planet for special effects usage.

The Return of the Archons

Director: Joseph Pevney

Writer: Boris Sobelman

1st Day of Filming: Tuesday, December 6, 1966   Last Day: Wednesday, December 14, 1966

Cost: $210,793   7 filming days

Slating a scene on the surface of planet Beta III, aka the Desilu 40 Acres lot in Culver City, California.

George Takei is slated for a close up shot in the Transporter Room on Day 1 while filming the teaser.

An unaired Lincoln film trim from the footage shot for the teaser on Day 1 - December 6, 1966.

Additional footage is captured on Day 3 on location at 40 Acres, on the same streets of Mayberry as used to film the planet bound scenes for "Miri".

Slating the arrival of Hacom and the lawgivers.

Harry Townes and Torin Thatcher in an unaired Lincoln film trim.

Bill McGovern slates a scene with Charles Macauley as Landru on Day 5.

A special effects shot features the projection of Landru about to interact with the landing party.

Space Seed

Director: Marc Daniels

Writer: Gene L. Coon and Carey Wilber

1st Day of Filming: Thursday, December 15, 1966   Last Day: Thursday, December 22, 1966

Cost: $197,262   6 filming days

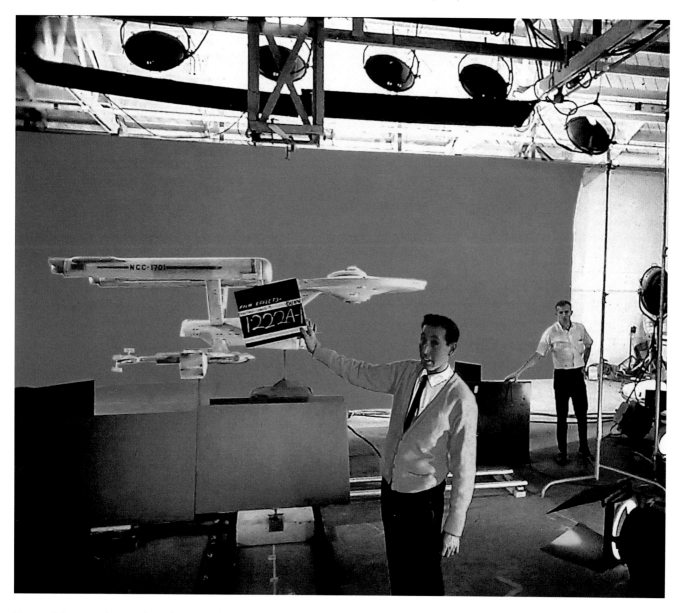

Barry Mason slates the shot as the 11' 2" U.S.S. Enterprise miniature is filmed alongside the smaller SS Botany Bay DY-100 class spacecraft model on the soundstage of Film Effects of Hollywood.

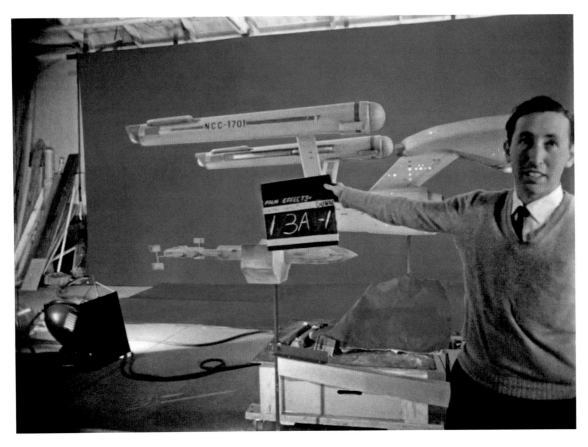

Some additional views of the Enterprise and Botany Bay models undergoing principal photography at Film Effects of Hollywood.

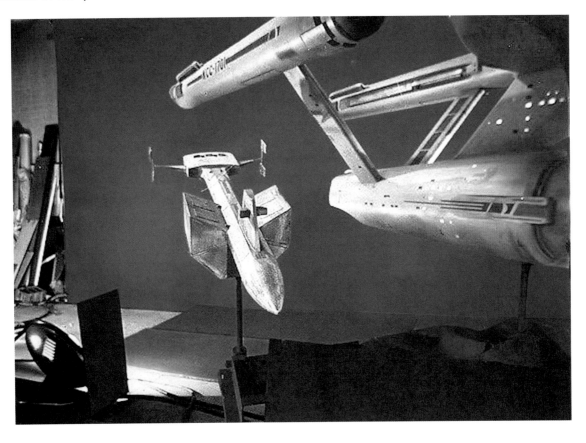

Slating a shot in the Briefing Room on Monday, December 19, 1966 - Day 3 of production.

Ricardo Montalban, in his iconic portrayal of the genetically-engineered superman Khan Noonien Singh, films a scene on Day 4 in the ship's Briefing Room.

In this rare NBC publicity shot, Ricardo Montalban is seen as Khan in an "old" 20th century-era photo from Earth, where - during a period in the mid-1990's - he presided as absolute ruler over more than one-quarter of the planet, from Asia to the Middle East.

On December 21st, Day 5 of production, Bill McGovern slates a shot of the Bridge crew's reaction upon seeing their Captain being tortured in the Decompression Chamber.

Filming the scene where Kirk crawls to safety out of the Medical Decom Chamber on Day 6.

The camera rolls in for a close up shot of the starship filming miniatures at Film Effects. Peering through the viewfinder of the Mitchell camera is Linwood G. Dunn, the main owner of the company and likely the preeminent special effects man of his time.

A Taste of Armageddon

Director: Joseph Pevney

Writer: Gene L. Coon and Richard Hamner

1st Day of Filming: Tuesday, December 27, 1966   Last Day: Wednesday, January 4, 1967

Cost: $194,108   6 filming days

David Opatoshu as Anan 7 in a deleted scene.

Just as it was utilized for the filming of "The Menagerie", a relatively small section of physical wall with accompanying statuary on Desilu Stage 10 was combined with a futuristic cityscape painting by Albert Whitlock to create, for this episode, the landing party beam down location on Eminiar VII.

Captain Kirk stands before the Eminian High Council in this unaired Lincoln film trim.

Bill McGovern slates a shot of Disintegration Chamber 12 in the Division of Control complex.

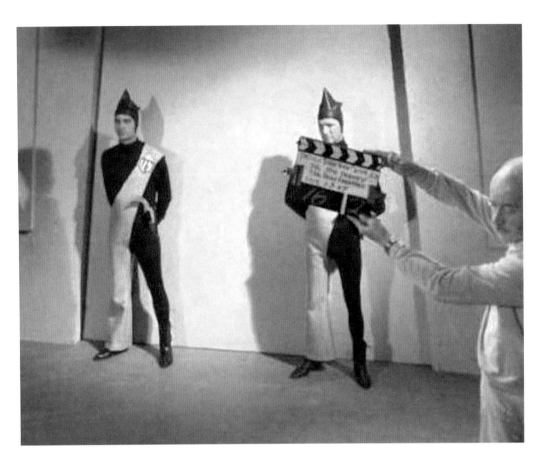

Slating a shot of two Eminian guards on Day 5 of production.

William Shatner is slated for a scene in the master computer room of Eminiar VII.

David Opatoshu and Gene Lyons, who portrayed Federation Ambassador Robert Fox, are slated for a close up shot on January 4, 1967 - the final day of production.

This Side of Paradise

Director: Ralph Senensky

Writer: D. C. Fontana

1st Day of Filming: Thursday, January 5, 1967

Cost: $171,681

Last Day: Friday, January 13, 1967

7 filming days

Leonard Nimoy and Jill Ireland pose for an NBC publicity photo on location at Bronson Canyon on the south edge of Griffith Park, in the Hollywood Hills.

Slating an opening scene on location at Disney Ranch, where the landing party encounters a very much alive group of Omicron Ceti III colonists led by Elias Sandoval, portrayed by Frank Overton.

A Lincoln film trim presents the same scene from an alternate camera angle, on Day 2 of production.

Above left, Jill Ireland in costume as Leila Kalomi, the botanist for the Omicron colony. Above right, Jill Ireland and Leonard Nimoy seen between takes at Desilu.

Nimoy and Ireland prepare to cross a small creek in these images from a deleted scene.

A rare shot of a completely empty Bridge set, just before Shatner enters from the turbolift.

A Lincoln clip from the heart-rending last scene between Spock and Leila in the Transporter Room.

Jill Ireland and Leonard Nimoy between takes on location at Bronson Canyon.

The Devil in the Dark

Director: Joseph Pevney

Writer: Gene L. Coon

1st Day of Filming: Monday, January 16, 1967   Last Day: Wednesday, January 25, 1967

Cost: $188,439   7 filming days

In this Lincoln film trim, Leonard Nimoy mind melds with the Horta - the first silicon based lifeform to appear on American network television.

The rare opening shot of the preview trailer for this episode, last publicly broadcast by NBC in 1967.

A Lincoln film trim featuring William Shatner with the matte painting visible in background.

An unaired Lincoln clip of the underground caverns in the mining colony on Janus VI, aka Desilu Stage 10. Note the perfectly smooth and polished cavern floors which stand in stark contrast to the roughly hewn walls. Gene Roddenberry took issue with these "stage-surface-like" floors, which he felt adversely impacted the believability of the set.

Slating a close up shot of the Horta on Thursday, January 19, 1967 - Day 4 of production.

Slating a shot on Day 4 with Eddie Paskey (photographed from the back) standing in for an absent William Shatner. The day before, Shatner had received a phone call on the set from his mother to notify him that his father had unexpectedly died while in Florida. He completed several scenes on Day 3 despite the tremendous pain and sorrow he was feeling, before flying out that evening.

Kirk and Spock prepare to encounter the Horta on the 5th filming day, and Shatner's first day back.

Slating a shot with Shatner and Ken Lynch as Chief Engineer Vandenberg on January 25, 1967 - Day 7.

The Horta's memorable message "NO KILL I" is captured in this Lincoln clip.

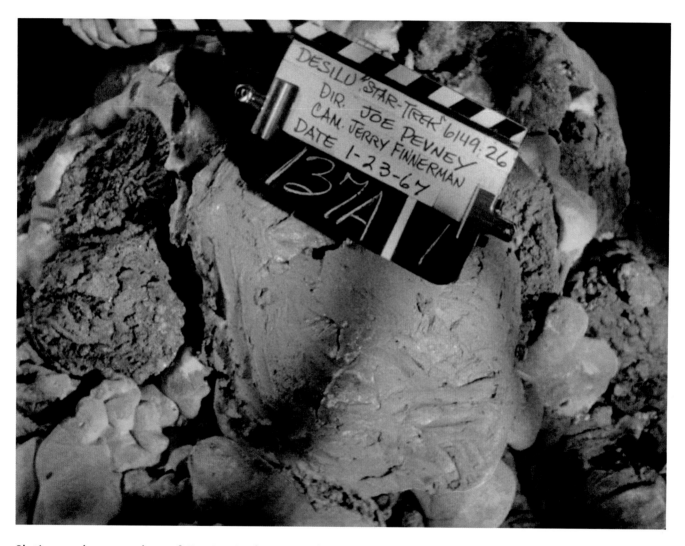

Slating a close up shot of Dr. McCoy's inspired medical handiwork in which he liberally applied one hundred pounds of thermal concrete to bandage the Horta's wound, despite protesting that he was "a doctor, not a bricklayer".

Errand of Mercy

Director: John Newland

Writer: Gene L. Coon

1st Day of Filming: Thursday, January 26, 1967

Last Day: Thursday, February 2, 1967

Cost: $175,527

6 filming days

John Abbott (second from right) appears as Ayelborne, the Chairman of the Council of Elders on the planet Organia, in this unaired Lincoln film trim.

William Shatner and Leonard Nimoy in a deleted scene from the episode.

Slating a shot of Nimoy at the Science Station on the Bridge on Friday, January 27, 1967 - Day 2.

175

An extraordinary image from the filming of the teaser which demonstrates how the TOS Bridge Set was ingeniously constructed as a series of removable pie shaped sections that could be repositioned as needed during production to facilitate the placement of camera and lighting equipment. Each pie section had independent electrical power switches, which were critical so that the section could be powered down by studio technicians immediately upon completion of the filming of a scene which involved that area of the Bridge set. This was necessary because most of the individual control panels and monitor displays in the various workstations were backlit by dozens of tiny 25-watt light bulbs, arranged in rows and wired to flash in desired sequences - and so panel overheating was a major concern at all times during production. It is fair to say the entire Bridge Set was virtually never fully illuminated at once - or if so - was fully lighted on only the rarest of occasions. For the broadcast version of the teaser being filmed above, of course, the wooden planks visible beneath the Bridge floor would be cropped out of view.

Some behind the scenes images while filming on location at Desilu 40 Acres. Director John Newland is visible at left in the above photo, while Script Supervisor George A. Rutter appears below at right.

John Colicos in his iconic role as Kor, the first and thus prototype Klingon.

A special effects shot that presents the Organians in their true form.

The City on the Edge of Forever

Director: Joseph Pevney

Writer: Harlan Ellison

1st Day of Filming: Friday, February 3, 1967   Last Day: Tuesday, February 14, 1967

Cost: $245,316   8 filming days

William Shatner and Joan Collins embrace in an NBC publicity photo. (Image colorized from B&W.)

Writer Harlan Ellison poses with Nimoy and Shatner during his visit to Desilu Stage 10 during the filming of the episode "Mudd's Women" in June, 1966.

Slating the shot for the climactic death of Edith Keeler while crossing the road in front of the mission. This scene was filmed on February 3, 1967 - the first day of production.

A moment of levity between takes as the cast films amongst the ruins of the Guardian planet on Stage 10, followed by a prompt resumption of composure as Bill McGovern arrives with his clapper.

Joan Collins folds a vintage lace tablecloth in a rare NBC publicity photo for this episode.

McGovern slates a shot of the Guardian of Forever, above; then Shatner, Nimoy, Nichols and Doohan appear in position before the time portal just a moment later, below.

In this behind the scenes image, DeForest Kelley prepares to film the re-emergence of Dr. McCoy through the time portal, back into his correct 23rd century time line, at the end of the episode ...

... as Bill McGovern slates a close up shot of the Guardian portal from the same camera angle on February 13, 1967 - Day 7 of production.

An endearing shot of Joan Collins on set in her iconic role as Edith Keeler.

Operation: Annihilate!

Director: Herschel Daugherty

Writer: Steven Carabatsos

1st Day of Filming: Tuesday, February 14, 1967   Last Day: Wednesday, February 22, 1967

Cost: $196,780   7 filming days

Leonard Nimoy, William Shatner, James Doohan and fellow landing party members fire on a number of the flying parasite creatures in this special effects shot. The production crew filmed this scene on location on Day 2 - Wednesday February 15, 1967 - at the TRW Defense and Space Group Campus in Redondo Beach, California; which is more familiar to viewers as the Federation colony on the planet Deneva.

Kelley, Shatner and Nimoy ham it up for the camera and pretend to shave with their hand phaser props during a break in filming at Redondo Beach.

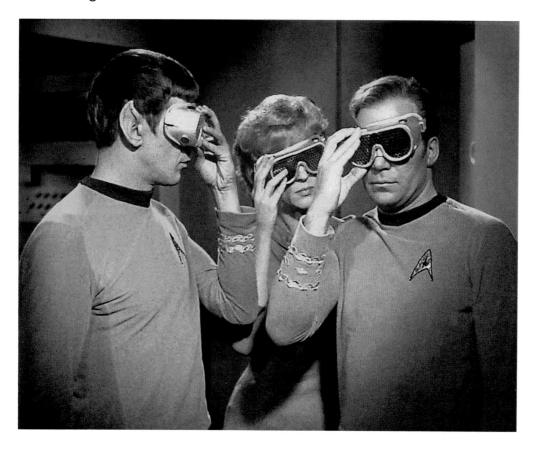

Leonard Nimoy, Majel Barrett and William Shatner try on protective googles in this unaired Lincoln film trim from Day 6 of production.

A close up shot of the neural parasite creature - one component of a giant single alien entity.

Some low resolution frames from a blooper reel, although of poor image quality, are still sufficient to capture a production crew joke at Nimoy's expense when a prop operator slams a flying parasite creature into the actors rear end instead of his upper back. Nimoy reacts in the bottom right frame.

A moment of levity while filming the landing party's first encounter with the Denevan colonists.

Craig Hundley, as Captain Kirk's nephew Peter Kirk, with William Shatner in a deleted "tag" scene.

NBC promotional photo to announce the Season 2 shift in timeslot.

Stay tuned ...

Made in the USA
Middletown, DE
14 June 2019